Business and society

Traditionally, managers have concentrated on co-ordinating the internal activities of their business. But the modern manager needs to be active on all interfaces between the business and the surrounding society. Today, managers who succeed are those who are able to appreciate and co-ordinate the work of many different specialists inside and outside the organization.

Business and Society examines the way in which business organizations interrelate with the communities in which they operate. Opening with a thorough discussion of the way business functions within a capitalist economy, the text then covers: basic business institutions, company law, tax laws, relations between the government and the private business sector, business ethics, business and the physical environment, business and technology, and people in business.

Edmund Marshall provides an authoritative account of topical issues linked with the more 'holistic' approach to business needed by today's manager and MBA student. The self-assessment exercises and exam questions he provides will be particularly useful for MBA Foundation Courses, as well as subsequent options on corporate governance and business strategy. This text will also be ideal for practising managers.

Edmund Marshall is Lecturer in Management Science at the University of Bradford Management Centre. He has had many years of experience working in industry and was a Labour Member of Parliament for twelve years. He is the author of *Parliament and the Public*.

Elements of Business Series
Series editor: David Weir
University of Bradford Management Centre

This important new series is designed to cover the core topics taught at MBA level with an approach suited to the modular teaching and shorter time frames that apply in the MBA sector. Based on current courses and teaching experience, these texts are tailor-made to the needs of today's MBA student.

Other titles in the series:

Management Accounting
Leslie Chadwick

Forthcoming:

Financial Accounting
Iain Campbell-Ward

Business Economics
John R. Sparkes, Bryan Lowes and Richard Welford

Managing Human Resources
C. Molander and J. Winterton

Business and society

Edmund Marshall

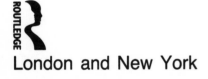

London and New York

First published 1993
by Routledge
11 New Fetter Lane, London EC4P 4EE

Simultaneously published in the USA and Canada
by Routledge
29 West 35th Street, New York, NY 10001

© 1993 Edmund Marshall

Phototypeset in Garamond by Intype, London
Printed and bound in Great Britain by
Mackays of Chatham PLC, Chatham, Kent

British Library Cataloguing in Publication Data
A catalogue reference for this book is available from the British Library

ISBN 0–415–06849–5 (hb)
      0–415–06850–9 (pb)

Library of Congress Cataloging in Publication Data
has been applied for

ISBN 0–415–06849–5 (hb)
      0–415–06850–9 (pb)

Contents

Figures

Preface

Postgraduate programmes for the degree of Master of Business Administration (MBA) are becoming increasingly popular in British institutions of higher education. The syllabuses of a growing number of such programmes include courses of study of the interrelationships between business management and the wider community, with titles like 'Society and Management', or 'The Business Environment'.

Students on such courses have been faced with a lack of suitable basic reading material relating to Business and Society. While there are obviously large numbers of good, up-to-date books on each of the individual topics included in these courses, there are very few texts covering the subject as a whole; nearly all that do relate to the American context. This book is therefore intended to provide a general introduction to the whole field of Business and Society. It is written not just as a students' textbook, but equally with present managers in mind, and much of the treatment of individual topics concentrates on the practical side of business management.

Inspiration for this book is drawn from the author's seven years' experience as co-ordinator of the Society and Management course on MBA programmes at the University of Bradford Management Centre, for both full-time and part-time students. On those courses I have personally given lectures on several of the different topics, and have listened to almost all the rest at some stage or other. Some of the chapters of the book have therefore been influenced indirectly by the contributions of academic colleagues and visiting lecturers at Bradford. In this context, acknowledgement is particularly due to Professors Tom Stonier and Kenneth Dyson and to Roger Fellows at Bradford University, to Timothy Wolstencroft and Howard Davies, law lecturers at Huddersfield Polytechnic and Leeds University respectively, to Guy Darby of N.M. Rothschild & Sons, Terry Goddard of MCL Technology Management, and to Stewart McCallum of Exxon Chemical Ltd. I am especially grateful to Tim Wolstencroft and Roger Fellows for providing me with the basic frameworks for Figures 3 and 4 respectively. The chapter on Business and Financial and Fiscal

Institutions was read by my colleague at the Management Centre, Bill Neale, who made several helpful criticisms and suggestions. Without all this help, the chapters on the subjects where I do not claim to have specialist knowledge or experience would have been impossible to write. Nevertheless, responsibility for all the contents of the book rests entirely with me; in writing it I have become all too aware of the difficulties involved in collating such a wide variety of topics.

It has been precisely these difficulties which have previously prevented the appearance of the book on this subject by a single author. At last that objective has now been attained, and I trust that the resulting book will be of interest and practical assistance to many present and future business managers.

Edmund Marshall
Management Centre, University of Bradford
June 1992

Chapter 1

Introduction

WHY MANAGERS NEED TO BE CONCERNED WITH SOCIETY

In 1889 the new soap factory of Lever Brothers Ltd was opened at Port Sunlight on the Wirral peninsula in Cheshire. The leading personality of the company was William H. Lever, later to become the first Viscount Leverhulme, one of the two brothers who were partners of the company, and one of the more progressive industrialists of his generation. The Port Sunlight works were carefully planned as the latest in industrial premises and were a major improvement on the previous premises of the company in the Bolton area of Lancashire. Around them was developed in the following years the whole model village of Port Sunlight, a residential community intended to house most of the employees of the factory. Lever became a legend for enlightened industrial management – his philanthropic interests extended to all aspects of the local community life and, for a few years, took him into Parliament as Member for the Wirral. In so many ways he came to be regarded as a model manager for his day, and his company grew in size and strength, becoming the basis for the modern multinational company, Unilever.

One feature of the new factory was particularly interesting, namely the position of Lever's own office within the building. Most of the general office area was constructed on an 'open plan' basis, and Lever's office was located high up, with glass walls to enable him to see all the workforce at their place of work (Jolly 1976: 31). Today, this would be regarded very much as Big Brother watching over his workers; but it is hardly likely that that was what Lever intended. Rather he was motivated by genuine altruism, having the interests of the workforce at heart. He saw the role of the good manager as one who knew exactly what was going on in all the operations of his business. For Lever, the business manager was the person who was truly at the hub of the organization and whose responsibility was to see that all the different parts of the business co-ordinated smoothly with one another. The manager's essential responsibility was to ensure the efficient relationship of each individual operation to the others, and to do this he was best located at the hub of the wheel of the whole organization.

Indeed, this is how managers of industrial and commercial enterprises in general have seen their role until recent times – namely as the kingpins of their organizations, holding them together and seeing that the activities of each part of the organization dovetailed smoothly with the rest.

The areas where external factors impinged most obviously on the running of the organization were levels of market demand, supply of materials and supply of labour. Classical economists had often encouraged business managers to take the view that these external factors were determined by the 'invisible hand' of market forces at work, and that the only way in which they could be influenced by the business manager was in the setting of prices and wage rates. If demand for a product dried up, or materials or labour became too expensive, then the business manager was traditionally brought to the conclusion that he had to change the activities of the firm or go out of business. He had to bow to the inevitable judgement of unseen market forces.

The first change in this attitude came when managers recognized that they could influence levels of demand for their products not only by alterations to price levels, but also by advertising. The advertising of products would make potential customers more aware of those products, and could win a larger share of the total market, either at the expense of competitors or by encouraging people to buy the goods who otherwise would not have bought at all. It was found that advertising became an essential commercial tool to stimulate demand, especially when the product was new or could be shown to differ significantly from competing products. For many commercial enterprises, advertising departments became the first really 'socially aware' departments of the organization, looking outwards from the firm and seeing how the mutual interaction between society and the firm could be changed. Managers who played an active role in the advertising function were thereby expressing concern with society outside the firm, and were recognizing that the interests of the firm required this outward-looking activity.

From advertising it was then a logical step to undertake market research. If a firm wished to influence the level of demand for its products, then it was important to know what products potential customers were most interested in buying, and what features of those products would most readily attract customers. Before a firm launched on the development of some new product, it was essential to gauge by market research how large a demand there would be for such a product, and how far that demand would be price-sensitive. By their very nature, market research departments in any commercial organization are oriented towards the outside community, and away from the processes in a firm devoted to production. But the good manager needed to be as much aware of all that was going on in his market research and advertising departments as in the production, distribution, accounts and other more traditional departments.

As a corollary of advertising and market research, it came to be recognized that the whole public standing of a business organization could affect its economic well-being. If a firm had a good reputation for the overall quality of its products, for its sympathetic handling of relationships with customers, for being a good employer or a good neighbour to those who lived close to its premises, then this standing would cause the general public to be more favourably disposed to buy the products of the firm. The whole field of public relations opened up to supplement advertising and market research, and grew in importance with the development of mass media and the growing interest of journalists and broadcasters in industrial and commercial matters.

The overall consequence of these developments has been that modern management is seen as a holistic activity – not just co-ordinating the processes of production and distribution, but looking at everything to do with the firm in its whole social context. Nothing that is related to a firm can be overlooked by its management, because it may have a bearing on the whole public perception and reputation of the firm and, in consequence, on its economic welfare. No longer are profits and losses regarded as being generated by unseen hands; they are the results of social trends and forces, which firms can often influence. If a firm is to succeed, and to maintain that success, every aspect of its existence has to be regarded as having a potential for good or ill in public esteem, which in turn will be reflected in profit or loss. Managers need to be concerned with society because it is from society alone that their firms can derive income, without which they cannot survive. 'Society' encompasses the very local area surrounding the firm's premises, the whole of the local town or area where employees live, and the whole of the area, national or international, where the firm's products are marketed or could be marketed and where its reputation is an essential aspect of its economic health.

THE HUB AND RIM OF THE ORGANIZATIONAL WHEEL

If then the role of the business manager is concerned increasingly with the relationship between his firm and society at large, and less on co-ordinating the internal functions of the business, his geographical position has shifted from the heart of the organization to the periphery. Rather than sitting in William Lever's glass-walled office in the middle of the factory, the modern manager needs to have a good external view through a panoramic window on the world. If the firm is shown diagrammatically, as in Figure 1, as a circle, then the manager's location is no longer fixed at the centre of the circle, but is increasingly at the perimeter. In the words of the former chairman and managing director of Standard Telephones and Cables plc:

> In discussing the manager of the future, it was . . . accepted . . . in the 1950s and 1960s he would have been located, diagrammatically, close to the centre of a circle which is his organization. At the periphery of the circle, where it met and joined with the external environment, would be the various staff people who performed the intelligence function of interpreting developments in the external environment for transmission to the centre for appropriate decision making. In the diagram for the 1980s, the manager is already at the periphery itself, managing the boundary conditions between the organisation and the constantly changing external environment. His new role is to match the capabilities and potentialities of the organisation with the potential and opportunities of the external environment. His functions are now more those of the negotiator, the interpreter, the politician, even the mediator, and decisions are made at the location closest to the action.
>
> (Corfield 1985: 3)

Figure 1 therefore shows the business organization as a wheel in which the location of the manager has moved from the hub to the rim. And around the rim are shown most, but not all, of the external factors which influence the boundary conditions of the organization.

The purpose of this book is to provide an introduction for those readers wishing to explore all these external factors bearing on the life of a business organization. The remainder of this section consists of a brief overview of all the topics to be covered in the following chapters, and is designed to give a view of the whole wood of Management and Society before embarking on a more detailed examination of individual trees. Essentially the social environment with which we are concerned is that applying to businesses in the United Kingdom, but the increasingly international nature of commercial activity means that that environment is continually being broadened, and many of the factors to be considered are applicable in many other countries, to a greater or lesser extent. Many of the factors present in the social environment of the United Kingdom, such as the system of government or the ethical climate, have been inevitably transferred to other countries within the Commonwealth and so are applicable there.

This is especially the case with the historical background to the development of business activity. Within any country there is an economic framework constructed by historical custom and practice, and the business manager needs to know broadly how that framework has come to be. The economy of the United Kingdom today is neither purely capitalist or purely socialist, and is sometimes described as a corporate, capitalist economy. The chief factors which have influenced the development of this economy will be reviewed in the next chapter. The economic and social

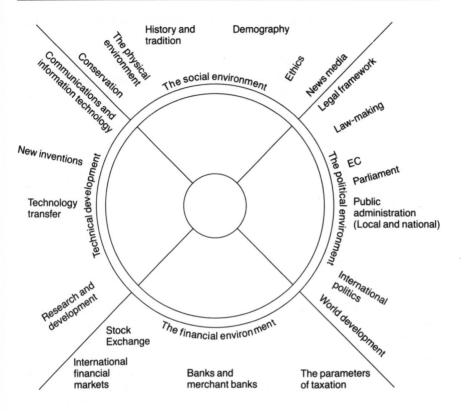

Figure 1 Boundary conditions of the modern business

framework for business is never static and continues to change, not least because of decisions by governments and public bodies, introducing new legislation and new administrative decrees and procedures. It is therefore important that business managers should understand how the processes of government operate and how those processes may be influenced by pressure exerted through the machinery of democracy, at local, national or European levels; in Chapter 3 this political environment will be examined more fully.

Many decisions of government and Parliament, past and present, are enforced through the legal courts of the land, and it is important that managers are conversant with the laws relating to their own businesses, and of how questions of law may be resolved through legal action in the courts. A review of the interaction between business and the law is given in Chapter 4, concentrating primarily on the system of courts in England

and Wales. While Scotland and Northern Ireland have their own legal jurisdictions with their own systems of courts, there is much legislation applicable throughout the whole of the United Kingdom.

In many respects, laws endeavour to interpret what public opinion deems to be the right way to act within the community, and this applies as much to business activity as to any other walk of life. So businesses are subject to the ethical climate of their social environment, and managers need to take stock of the ethical standards of society. These ethical standards may be expressed in codes of practice as well as in legal statutes, but they are also evident in public opinion, which firms may be reluctant to alienate. There are different kinds of ethics; in Chapter 5 we shall describe the influence that they have on business activity.

One area of government which closely affects the operation of any business is that of taxation, which is administered by the Inland Revenue and the tax-gathering office for value added tax, HM Customs and Excise. These are two of the financial institutions which are influential in the whole business and industrial sector, others being the London Stock Exchange, the merchant banks and investment houses, particularly in view of the growing significance within the economy of institutional investors. The roles of these financial institutions are considered more fully in Chapter 6.

Almost irrespective of politics, economics and ethics, much business activity is influenced by technological developments. Most large firms today have research and development departments or programmes, and technical innovation is often a major factor in commercial success, both in the development of new products and in terms of the *modus operandi* of businesses themselves. New inventions have led to commercial revolutions, and the processes of technology transfer are important for most businesses. Perhaps the revolutions most widely experienced in business management in recent years have related to information technology, communications and the electronic transfer of funds. In Chapter 7 the impact of technological development on business organizations is described in more detail.

Not only is the social environment of business constantly changing in political and ethical terms, but the nature of people making up that social environment never stands still. The age cross-section of the population in any one country varies as people live longer, or as the birth rate alters, or as a generation is depleted by the ravages of war or famine. The pattern of economic activity will vary because different age-groups require different goods or services, and the labour market will change because of earlier retirement or because more women wish to pursue careers. Demographic factors like these are considered in Chapter 8, and need to be built into the planning of any successful business organization.

We saw earlier how it was the development of public relations activities of businesses which brought managers away from the hubs and nearer to the rims of their organizations. In some senses, all of Management and Society can be regarded as the exercise of public relations, but usually the term PR relates to the more specific relationships which a business has with the local community, with news media and with government, either locally or nationally. Chapter 9 describes some of the activity which comes under the heading of PR, whether it is carried out internally by staff employed by a firm or externally by PR consultants.

One field which has become increasingly important for business managers in recent years is the impact which their firms' activities have on the physical environment, and attention is given to this in Chapter 10. In part this relates to the impact which technology has on the environment, in part it relates to the pressure of public opinion and the expression of ethical views about the physical environment, and in part it involves compliance with legislation on pollution control and protection of the environment. Much of the impact which commercial activity has on the physical environment has to be viewed in global terms, through depletion of world resources or through atmospheric pollution and factors such as damage to the ozone layer. World conservation and development are further items now appearing on the agenda of Management and Society.

THE ULTIMATE AIMS OF A BUSINESS

In the light of all this, many business managers may feel that they have a herculean task, that they cannot possibly keep abreast of all these factors bearing upon their own organizations. Some may well wonder whether it is worth all the effort and expense involved in being properly socially oriented. They may ask why they should bother about society at large. Surely their responsibility is to their own firms, to their employers and to their shareholders? Should not everything be measured by the bottom line of profit or loss, and will not bothering about the various social implications reduce the level of profit (or increase the level of loss)? They may protest that it is not their job to worry about social factors and that there are politicians or clergymen or journalists to do that. They may claim that it is not in the interests of their businesses to give way to all these social pressures and that their one overriding purpose must be to maximize the financial gain of their respective firms.

Increasingly, however, firms have discovered that their interests are jeopardized if they do not take account of these social factors. This has been the experience particularly of large organizations, dependent on widespread public esteem and support. If they do not act in accordance with the law, if they lose cases in the courts, and if they fail to influence the passage of new legislation, they can suffer financially, sometimes catastrophically so. If they do not keep up with technological changes, they will be outstripped by their competitors. If they ignore public opinion, their public image will be undermined to the extent of lost business and reduced economic performance. If they damage the environment or exhaust raw material supplies, they may contribute in the long term to their own demise and to the impoverishment of future generations. So, in all these ways, a business manager is acting in his firm's best interests if he takes proper account of the social environment and reacts positively to the boundary conditions of his organization.

In some quarters of the business world, this has been recognized by the concept of the stakeholder in a firm, as opposed to the traditional stockholder, or shareholder. Stakeholders include anyone who has an interest in the operations of the firm: employees, customers, neighbourhood groups, environmental pressure groups, even politicians. Proponents of the stakeholder concept argue that the decisions of boards of directors should take into consideration the interests of all stakeholders, in order to maximize the overall level of satisfaction with the firm, and that in the long term the best interests of the stockholders will thereby be served.

All this boils down to the simple question of why a business is in existence. If the answer is simply to make money, to maximize the financial return to the owners of the business, then the supplementary question immediately arises as to who is going to provide that money. Since it is the customer who provides the income, then clearly the wishes of the customer become part of the interests of the stockholder. The old business adage that 'the customer is always right' goes some way to recognizing this confluence of the interests of producers and customers, and today trade depends not only on the goodwill of immediate customers but on the whole public reputation of the firm. Consequently a firm will be in a better position to maximize its financial return if it takes full account of the interests of all stakeholders. The stockholder is best served if the stakeholders are all happy.

In practical terms it can therefore be claimed that a successful business exists to serve the community as a whole. The better it serves the community, the more it will flourish. The adoption of an ethical standpoint in society will best advance the self-interest of the individual firm. Those with a more high-minded view of ethics will claim that service of the community is really the primary aim of business, and the accumulation of profit is simply a measurement of how successful a firm is in serving the community. Whatever may be the ethical standpoint of the individual business manager, it is clear that his role in contemporary business is to interact positively all round the rim of his organization and to operate in the best interests of society as a whole. His office must have good external windows providing a comprehensive view of all the surrounding community.

Let us then look through those windows one by one.

Chapter 2

The current corporate, capitalist economy

THE CLASSICAL ECONOMISTS AND *LAISSEZ-FAIRE*

A fundamental influence on the business organizations of any community is the economic structure determined by the general state of morality, practice and law in that community. In this chapter consideration is given to the various ingredients which have contributed during the last four centuries to the development of the economy of the United Kingdom. Such contributions have come from philosophers, from politicians, from technical innovators and from the general climate of public opinion. No single contributory factor has been dominant, with the result that the current economy of this country is truly a mixed economy, in contrast with some other countries where one factor alone has predominated, largely as a result of political circumstances. In the UK the continued political success of Conservative governments since 1979 has made the economy less mixed now than it was then.

The origins of the modern British economy are usually traced to the so-called 'classical' economists of the late eighteenth and early nineteenth centuries, men of academic and business backgrounds who observed what was happening as the Industrial Revolution unfolded. The doyen of the classical economists is almost universally regarded as Adam Smith, a Scot born in Fife in 1723 who spent most of his life as an academic member of Glasgow University, with major interests in logic, moral philosophy, politics and law; Smith was not a specialist economist in the modern sense. His major work, *An Inquiry into the Nature and Causes of the Wealth of Nations*, nowadays generally abbreviated to the last four words, which was published in 1776, examined the consequences of economic freedom such as division of labour, market mechanisms and exchanges, especially in the context of colonial empires and international trade. Smith's views were by no means as precise as his later disciples liked to claim, although his book had an immediate impact and influence, not least on the man soon to become prime minister for twenty years, William Pitt.

Another disciple of Adam Smith was a young and successful stockbroker, David Ricardo, whose interest in political economy was aroused by reading *The Wealth of Nations* in 1799. His own major contribution to economic thinking appeared in 1817, entitled *The Principles of Political Economy and Taxation*, which discussed values, wages and rent, among other subjects. From 1819 until his death in 1823 Ricardo was a Radical Member of Parliament.

Some of Ricardo's main work was anticipated in 1815 by the publication of *An Inquiry into the Nature and Progress of Rent* by the Revd Thomas Malthus, a clergyman who had become Professor of political economy at the East India College at Haileybury in 1805. Malthus had earlier published his *Essay on the Principle of Population*, in 1798, in which he attempted to apply the principles of the free market to the size of the population. In that work, Malthus argued that it is inevitable that the natural growth of population will outstrip the growth of the provision of food, and therefore that poverty will always be present, limiting the population by starvation.

These and other classical economists put forward the free market philosophy that the balance between demand for a commodity and its supply is achieved automatically through the price mechanisms of the market. If there is no demand for a commodity, no one will pay a price for it, so no income is available for any supplier. On the other hand, if demand for a product increases, then customers will be prepared to pay a higher price for it, which will encourage suppliers to produce more. Market equilibrium is achieved by the price mechanism when supply is equal to demand. Demand in the community is best met by producers whose goods command the highest prices, so the producer best serves the community by acting with intent to maximize his own financial return. This doctrine of enlightened self-interest involved the acceptance of a 'natural order' of economic affairs in which the 'invisible hand' of the market would itself regulate supply to equate with demand.

These ideas were taken up and developed by others during the nineteenth century, notably by John Stuart Mill, the civil servant and Utilitarian philosopher, who is best remembered for his essay *On Liberty*, published in 1859. Mill argued that, if the community was best served by businesses which sought to maximize their own financial return, then it was necessary for them to have the widest possible political freedom for their operations. Economic and personal freedom should be extended as widely as possible to allow self-interest to operate freely, and intervention by governments or by statutory action should be absent. This is the doctrine of *laissez-faire*, the theory that industrialists and business operators should be left alone to get on with their activities, free of legal, political or fiscal encumbrance, in order most effectively to meet the needs of the community. (Note that, in the name of this doctrine, *laissez* sometimes takes a final 'r', depending on which form of the verb fits the particular context.)

Mill's ideas were widely influential in government circles in the 1860s, and it is of interest that he was himself elected to Parliament in 1865 to serve for three years as a 'working-man's representative'.

At the same time, however, the nature of business organization in Britain was undergoing fundamental change in another direction, as described in later sections of this chapter. Suffice to say here that the business organizations observed by the classical economists were of a totally different nature from the general business company observed today. Most of them were small, family concerns, managed and operated by their owners, with very few shareholders outside the families of the firms' principals. This was because, up to the 1840s and 1850s, most businesses were partnerships of shareholders; very few companies had a legal entity of their own. Furthermore, the absence of limited liability before 1856 meant that individual citizens were reluctant to invest their savings in companies when such investments made them totally liable to meet any successful claim against those companies. The business scene addressed by the classical economists prior to the middle of the nineteenth century underwent a sea change at that time; so the applicability of their free market philosophy in later years, including today, needs to be treated with care.

We must now turn to examine how the sea change of the mid-Victorian period came about.

The growth of the joint-stock company

Prior to 1844 the only business companies in the United Kingdom with a corporate legal entity were those which possessed a royal charter or which had been incorporated by private Act of Parliament. All other businesses, no matter how many shareholders they had, were simply partnerships of those shareholders, and could sue or be sued in the courts of law only in actions which listed all the shareholders as joint parties. In such cases a business could bring a case to court only if all the partners were in agreement about taking the action, while on the other hand another party could sue such a business only by bringing an action against all the shareholders equally and jointly. These legal impediments strongly discouraged businesses from attracting more than a few shareholders, although at the same time they deterred the taking of legal action against a firm with many shareholders.

Such restrictions did not apply to companies established by charter granted by the monarch of the day, for by such charter they were given corporate status and could sue or be sued as bodies corporate. The earliest such company was the Muscovy Company of Merchant Adventurers, which was granted a royal charter by King Edward VI in 1553 to develop trade links with Russia by the northern sea route to Archangel (Churchill 1956: 74). In the remaining decades of the Tudor period several more companies were given charters: the Cathay Company in 1577 to further exploration of the north-west passage tentatively explored by Martin Frobisher, the Turkey Company of 1581 which in 1592 joined forces with the Venice Company to form the Levant Company, which traded successfully in the Eastern Mediterranean for two centuries, and, the most famous of all, the East India Company, founded in 1600. As colonization in North America developed during the seventeenth century, the Stuart kings granted more charters, to the Virginia Company in 1606, to the Massachusetts Bay Company in 1628 and to the Hudson's Bay Company in 1670.

While these corporate bodies traded with varying degrees of success, either in promoting colonial settlement or in achieving financial profit, the same could hardly be said of the South Sea Company, formed in 1710 to trade with Spanish America. Although this company was boosted in 1713 when it received the sole right, granted in the Treaty of Utrecht that year, to supply slaves to Spanish colonies, it overstretched itself in 1720 with a plan to absorb the whole of the national debt. In a climate of political scandal and intrigue, both Houses of Parliament agreed to this scheme. The soaring popularity of owning shares in the company pushed up their price eightfold. The slump followed even more quickly, between June and December 1720, when the share price returned to near its original level, leaving thousands of people ruined, with many suicides, including that of the Postmaster-General (Churchill 1957: 93–4). The government fell in chaos, and Sir Robert Walpole stepped in to begin his twenty-one years as prime minister.

The South Sea Bubble, as it came to be called, was perhaps the incident in which a single business company had the most impact in history on the whole of national life. Ministers took action to see that the experience would never be repeated. Legislation, in the form of the Bubble Act of 1720, was passed to impose restrictions on the organization of joint-stock companies and to prohibit all such companies without incorporation granted by either royal charter or Act of Parliament. The Bubble Act was not repealed until 1825 and applied a very firm brake on economic and industrial development for over a century. And it was during that century that the ideas of the classical economists gained ground.

In these circumstances it is not surprising that many businesses sought incorporation by private Acts of Parliament, especially insurance companies during the time of the Napoleonic wars and railway companies from the 1820s onwards. Parliament enacted no less than 100 such Acts between 1802 and 1844, and the procedures for such legislation occupied a large proportion of the time of both Houses throughout much of the nineteenth century.

The repeal of the Bubble Act in 1825 legalized unincorporated companies as partnerships, without giving them legal entity, and it also increased the power of the Crown to prescribe a 'regulated' liability for incorporated companies, instead of unlimited liability (*vide* Jones and Pool 1940: 132). Much more important was the Registration Act of 1844, which introduced the registration of joint-stock companies in England and Wales which were not banks and which had more than twenty-five members holding transferable shares; registration conferred legal entity on such companies, but the liability of shareholders remained unlimited and continued for a period of three years after any shareholder sold his interest.

The impact of limited liability

During the 1850s the pressure for the granting of limited liability to registered companies increased as the business sector sought to expand and attract capital from a wider circle of shareholders. Limited liability was already in operation in other countries, which were therefore able to attract British capital. On the other hand it was recognized that in principle limited liability was a form of legal protection contrary to the whole spirit of *laissez-faire* which then dominated economic and political thinking.

These tensions were resolved in 1856 when the government, in which Palmerston was prime minister and Robert Lowe was President of the Board of Trade, introduced the parliamentary Bill which became the Limited Liability Act 1856. Under this legislation a limited company other than a bank or insurance company could be formed by seven or more investors signing a memorandum of association declaring the name and aims of the company. Similar provisions were extended to banks in a further Act of 1858, and to insurance companies in the Companies Act of 1862, which also consolidated the previous enactments.

This legislation paved the way for rapid development of joint-stock companies during the 1860s. In 1864, for example, 975 companies were registered, with a nominal capital of £235 millions, and the number grew for most of the rest of the century. There was of course the danger that limited liability would be abused, as the Master of the Rolls at the time said, to promote companies for the sole purpose of their being wound up, whereby the capital subscribed by gullible investors could be squandered by promoters and lawyers before bankruptcy ensued. Of the first five thousand limited companies formed between 1856 and 1865, no less than 36 per cent had ceased to exist within five years, and 54 per cent within seven years, of their promotion (Jones and Pool 1940: 135). The conversion of old businesses into limited companies was slow, but hastened in the 1880s, with over 500 such conversions taking place between 1880 and 1885. In textiles, cutlery and even in shipping, businesses remained in established private hands until late in the century. It was in other sectors, including steel, chemicals, railways and insurance, that vast expansions of commercial activity occurred, particularly where new industrial processes were capital intensive.

Limited liability attracted the capital required for vast industrial and commercial expansion, with the growth of British trade world-wide and throughout the Empire. In turn these international links fostered the development of multinational organizations, with overseas subsidiary companies wholly owned by parent companies at home, which might be little more than holding companies. The pattern developed for the kind of capitalism and private enterprise which has played a leading role in the British economy for most of the twentieth century. Such capitalism was markedly different from the free enterprise economy of Adam Smith, largely because of limited liability, which was the deliberate introduction by politicians of protective restriction on the forces of the free market. Since 1862 investors in public companies in the United Kingdom have enjoyed an element of legal protection in the form of limited liability which runs counter to the philosophy of *laissez-faire*.

The growth in the number of individual shareholders and in the size of businesses led to a widening gap between company ownership and company management. More and more businesses were run by their boards and by employed management, while the contributions of other shareholders were restricted to buying and selling their shares, receiving dividends, and attending and voting at company annual meetings. The typical business ceased to be the family firm, owned and run by a few related individuals, but instead became the large company with perhaps a few major shareholders who were also on the board of directors, and many thousands of other passive shareholders, scattered far and wide. In general there was a marked transfer to power in such business corporations, from the owners to the managers. The prevalent form of capitalist organization became less the *laissez-faire* business of the individual entrepreneur, and more the large corporate private company.

THE DEVELOPMENT OF GOVERNMENT INTERVENTION

During the first three-quarters of the twentieth century the prevailing trend in the structure of the British economy was the increased involvement of central government and other public authorities and the increased influence of legal requirements and constraints. For a wide variety of reasons it was decided by successive governments that the economy should not be left fully for the free market to regulate, but that there should be growing involvement by central and local government and more influence exerted on businesses by fiscal policy and statutory constraints. These trends were by no means unique to this country, and indeed other nations operated much more controlled economies, through state socialism or communism. While the UK economy remained mixed, the dominant trend from the

early years of the twentieth century until 1979 was a strengthening of
public involvement in the economy, with correspondingly less reliance on
the interplay of free market forces.

One way in which this trend came about was through the enactment
by Parliament of more and more legislation imposing statutory duties and
powers on business and companies and individuals. This use of statute
law to influence economic activities was nothing new. For almost as long
as Parliament has been in existence, it has had the opportunity to introduce
laws affecting the economic activities of private citizens and groups. For
instance, as long ago as 1570, in the reign of Elizabeth I, Parliament
enacted legislation requiring every member of the 'lower classes' over the
age of six to wear a wool cap on Sundays and public holidays (13 Eliz.,
c. 19). This legislation was obviously introduced under pressure from the
influential wool interests represented in Parliament, and represents a degree
of statutory involvement in economic affairs and in people's individual
lives which would not be tolerated today. But this is only one example
of how in Tudor England political power was openly used to influence
the pattern of economic activity. The mercantile system which dominated
the pattern of trade in most of Western Europe during Tudor and Stuart
times provided many opportunities for princes, rulers and parliaments to
exercise power in economic affairs.

During the nineteenth century legislation was increasingly used to regulate economic activities. While the prevailing economic philosophy
remained *laissez-faire*, even so humanitarian pressures in Parliament
brought about the end of the slave trade, the end of the employment in
coal-mines of children under the age of thirteen and of women by the
Mines Act of 1842, and the gradual improvement of conditions of employment in factories generally, by a succession of Factory Acts. In 1865 the
Alkali Inspectorate was formed to monitor gaseous and liquid emissions
from industrial premises, becoming the forerunner of today's pollution
control machinery. These and many other examples show how the British
system of parliamentary democracy, driven by a steadily widening franchise, brought about more and more legislation which regulated and constrained the activities of commerce and industry.

That process accelerated throughout the twentieth century, partly with
the coming of universal adult suffrage and partly with the growing readiness of the press and other mass media to report and expose any business
activities generally considered not to be in the public interest. Ministers
in governments of all shades of political opinion might find themselves
under pressure from the public and from parliamentary representatives to
introduce or amend legislation to control or constrain almost any area of
economic life. For example, when in the 1980s certain makes of children's
dolls were found to contain dangerous spikes, a public outcry and widespread publicity led a minister in a Conservative government to promise

new legislative controls to prevent the future manufacture of similar dangerous toys. There is no doubt that the existence of democratic pressures within the UK political system makes it inevitable that today there is a steady flow of legislation introducing more and more controls to counter or modify the effects of free market forces. Parliamentary democracy is hardly compatible with a pure market economy. The result is a formidable measure of public involvement within our system of free enterprise.

In addition, the effect on economic activity of other types of legislation, primarily intended for other purposes, has nonetheless been considerable. This applies in particular to the effects on commerce and industry of much taxation policy. When governments have needed to raise revenue to finance their spending programmes, the fiscal methods employed have often had far-reaching effects on economic activity. Taxes imposed upon goods, such as purchase tax, VAT, car tax or petrol duty, have inevitably influenced the levels of demand for those goods. Import duties have distorted the impact of free competition of goods from overseas. Payroll taxes, such as the employers' contributions to national insurance, increase the cost of labour and can have drastic effects on the employment market. Corporation taxes clearly alter the profitability of companies. In ways like these, taxation introduced to provide the government with the revenue it requires has far-reaching effects on economic activity. It is to be hoped that politicians take full account of these effects in making taxation proposals – and indeed sometimes they may see those effects as being socially desirable – but again the impact of such fiscal measures is a further distortion of the free market economy.

During the middle part of the twentieth century it became fashionable for UK governments of various political persuasions to use budgeting policy to achieve desired political and social objectives. The influential work of the Cambridge economist J. M. Keynes during the 1920s and 1930s encouraged governments to tackle the problems of economic depression and mass unemployment by deliberately budgeting for national deficits, thereby increasing the flow of money into the economy and stimulating demand. In the United States during the same period the New Deal policies of President Roosevelt pumped massive amounts of money into public works programmes, such as the Tennessee Valley Authority hydro-electricity scheme, in order to create employment and stimulate demand in the economy. Such policies represented massive public intervention in the economy. They were impelled by a political conviction that solutions had to be found to the problems of depression and unemployment, and that the free enterprise economy was incapable of providing such solutions. After the Second World War Keynesian thinking dominated the economic policies of both left and right in British politics through to the 1970s. Then the persistence of another economic problem, inflation, led to the Keynesian approach being questioned, and to a complete change of economic policies in the 1980s, as described later. For some forty years, however, the adoption by UK governments of Keynesian economic policies constituted a major public involvement in the economy.

At the same time there was a steady extension of the machinery of government, in pursuit of social and political objectives. Not only was the Civil Service constantly expanded in size, but many other statutory and semi-official bodies were introduced by governments to carry through statutory duties or oversee other aspects of the nation's economic life. Some of these became known as 'quangos', quasi non-governmental organizations, and many of them exercised considerable influence in the economy. At the national level, they included the National Economic Development Council, 'Neddy', which continues to provide a forum for the discussion of the economic problems of the nation. 'Neddy' includes representation from government, in the form of six senior cabinet ministers, from the Confederation of British Industry and from the Trades Union Congress, as well as having other independent members. 'Neddy' also produced a family of 'little neddies', or subcouncils relating to specific sectors of the economy. Other quangos included the regional development councils and consumer consultative committees for specific industries, particularly in the public sector. Sections of government departments were hived off as separate organizations, such as the Manpower Services Commission, while other long-established bodies were remodelled and extended, such as the Health and Safety Executive. Such organizations so easily generate further expansion of their own, with bureaucracy taking charge and adopting an attitude of protection towards the organization itself. It is therefore debatable to what degree such bodies help or hinder economic development; but there is no doubt that many of them have had a far-reaching impact on the pattern of economic activity.

In other cases new government machinery was introduced deliberately to intervene in commercial and industrial affairs. The system of town and country planning, introduced by legislation from 1947 onwards, imposed a whole series of controls on new development and on change of land use; the need to obtain planning permission for new factories and processes was relaxed only with the introduction of enterprise zones in the 1980s. At one stage all industrial development was controlled by a system of certificates allocated on a regional basis, and under successive Industry Acts financial incentives were available to encourage new industrial construction or the provision of new plant.

Equally interventionist was the machinery introduced by the Monopolies and Restrictive Practices Act of 1948 and by subsequent legislation to take the initiative in investigating whether mergers and take-overs of companies were in the public interest, and to counter monopoly situations. The present Monopolies and Mergers Commission is able to consider whether merger proposals are in the public interest and, if not, to advise the relevant government minister to prevent them. Such action is of course in direct opposition to the free market philosophy, but it is generally accepted across the whole political spectrum as being socially beneficial.

Perhaps the most significant development of public intervention in the economy during the twentieth century has been the growth of public ownership, with the legal possession of the means of economic production, distribution and exchange being vested in public authority, either in government itself, or in a public board specially constituted for that purpose by Parliament, or in a local authority. By no means can all public ownership be attributed to the practice of particular party politics, and there are at least four different strands of motivation which can be identified from all the instances of public ownership to date.

One of the earliest industries to be publicly owned was the Post Office. From the earliest days of the public mail services, it was recognized that ownership of the mail was vested in the monarch of the day – hence the term 'Royal Mail'. With the introduction of the penny post in 1840 and the consequent expansion of the mail business, the Post Office was set up as a government department presided over by a minister, the Postmaster-General, whose duties were thereby considerably extended. There was no question at that time but that this community service was rightly to be regarded as part of the public domain, and its operations part of the public service. In later years, there were other community services where it was generally regarded as right for public ownership to apply, such as the provision of water by water boards or by water departments of local authorities. Because such services were available for use by all members of the public, they were provided at standard rates of charge and it was generally accepted as appropriate that their ownership should be in public hands.

Governments also came to believe that the strategic importance of other sectors and organizations in the economy meant that they were sensibly owned by government or by boards directly responsible to government. Such strategic considerations applied to the telephone system and to the gas and electricity industries. And in the aftermath of the Second World War the important role played in the British economy by the Bank of England made that organization a suitable candidate for nationalization, which came about in 1946. This enabled the Chancellor of the Exchequer to have much closer control through the Governor over the operations of the Bank in the steering of national economic policy. Although in many respects the Bank of England appears to be a major bastion of the free market economy, it has in fact been completely publicly owned since 1946, and until very recently there had been few suggestions that it should be otherwise.

Many other extensions of public ownership have been overtly due to the implementation of party political programmes. One of the first instances of this was the public ownership of London Transport in 1933, brought about through the democratically elected Labour majority on the London County Council under the leadership of Herbert Morrison, who had been Minister of Transport in the Labour government of 1929–31. The London Passenger Transport Board served as a model for the later boards of nationalized industries which were introduced by the Labour government of 1945 to assume ownership of the nation's coal-mines in 1947, of the railways in 1948, and so on. Some of these acts of nationalization were spurred on by an intense longing to redistribute the power within an industry on general humanitarian grounds, or by other deeply held political convictions. To achieve public ownership and control of the commanding heights of the economy was one of the objects written into the Labour Party constitution in 1918. The establishment of the National Health Service in 1948 extended public ownership in the service sector of the economy.

But Labour governments were not the only ones to extend public ownership. While the steel and road transport industries became the objects of games of political ping-pong, passing in and out of public ownership as government succeeded government, the main programme of nationalization carried through by the Labour government of 1945 was not dismantled by the Conservative administrations which followed in the 1950s, 1960s and 1970s. Indeed the 1970 Conservative government of which Mr Heath was prime minister extended public ownership to companies where there was a major national interest at stake, such as International Computers Ltd, or where there was a threat that a company of major national importance might go bankrupt, such as Rolls-Royce or British Leyland. The rescue of 'lame-duck' companies thus became a further reason for extension of public ownership.

In these ways the programme of public ownership between 1945 and 1979 added very considerably to public involvement in the running of the economy. While the economy remained decidedly mixed, throughout the twentieth century up to 1979 there was a steady advance in the public sector and in public influence over the economy. In 1979, however, the tide turned abruptly.

THE PRIVATIZATION PROGRAMME OF THE 1980s

The election on 3 May 1979 of the Conservative government of which Mrs Thatcher was prime minister proved to be a major watershed in the whole life of the nation, particularly in relation to economic activity. Keynesian economic thought was replaced by 'monetarism', whereby there would be strong Treasury control of the supply of money to the economy, with the aim of overcoming inflation, which at times had been running at over 20 per cent during the 1970s. As part of this strategy, it was seen that the public sector borrowing requirement would be reduced if many of the organizations in public ownership could be transferred to private hands; then the need for those organizations to raise capital could be met on the open market, rather than through government borrowing. To some extent this reduction in PSBR was a book-keeping measurement, but it served to bolster international confidence in sterling, and of course the monies paid by shareholders for their shares in the newly privatized companies helped to swell Treasury funds.

At the same time the return of these organizations to the private sector helped to reduce the amount of political responsibility carried by government. No matter how little ministers might wish to be involved in the day-to-day operations of the nationalized industries, the fact that they were in public ownership and were answerable to Parliament through the relevant ministers meant that in many ways governments could not avoid 'carrying the can' for these organizations; privatization removed that responsibility. It is of interest that the widespread increases in the rates of pay for chairmen of the newly privatized companies in the early 1990s have been widely criticized, but in all cases government ministers have been able to say, correctly, that these matters are no longer in their field of responsibility.

Just as earlier Labour governments had overt political grounds for extending public ownership, so the Conservative governments of the 1980s had ample political motive for returning organizations to private shareholders. And the more shareholders the better. Whenever public interest in a share issue has been oversubscribed, the government has invariably favoured small shareholders, so as to maximize the total number of shareholders in the country. This was partly in furtherance of the Conservative objective of a property-owning democracy, and partly to boost support for the Conservatives among the electorate. The more people who were owning shares, the less likely they would be to vote Labour and risk the loss or devaluing of their newly acquired assets. From this point of view the privatization policy can be seen as a party political coup, contributing to Conservatives victories in successive general elections.

And so throughout the 1980s the privatization programme rolled on. Companies which had been rescued by public ownership were returned to private hands: Rolls-Royce, Jaguar, British Leyland; other organizations which had long been publicly owned – British Telecom, British Gas, British Steel, British Airways, BAA, the water authorities and the electricity companies, were all successfully sold off. In only one case was privatization a flop, namely the sale of the remaining government shareholding in British Petroleum, the selling price of which was fixed just before the stock market crash of October 1987, and which therefore failed to attract sufficient investors. The programme continues unabated, and it would appear that there is still much more to come, possibly including British Rail and British Coal, at least so long as a government of the same political complexion remains in power.

But these privatized companies are in general very different from the model of the private enterprise company which operated prior to the Second World War. In the case of many of them, where a monopoly or near-monopoly public service is provided, the new company is now strictly subject to monitoring by a regulatory body, such as OFTEL in the case of telecommunications, OFGAS in the case of British Gas, or OFWAT for the water companies. These regulatory bodies have been established by statute with powers to ensure that the companies operate in the public interest. With such regulation, one cannot say that these companies are operating in a free market economy.

In this chapter the main ingredients contributing to the current state of the corporate capitalist economy in the UK have been considered, with the picture brought up to date. But of course that picture is ever-changing, and any assessment of the economic climate within which a business operates needs constant updating. One reason why managers need to be more aware of what is happening in society at large is the fast-changing nature of that scene. Survival in modern business is only possible if a company can be adapted quickly to match all the changing conditions of its business environment. The historical survey undertaken in this chapter may be of value only as a basis for appreciating the continuously changing economic and political environment as it develops. Much of the skill of modern management is the skill of managing change in a rapidly changing world. In the following chapters we shall consider the various aspects involved in that changing scene today.

Chapter 3

Business and government

THE IMPORTANCE OF DECISIONS BY PUBLIC AUTHORITY

In the previous chapter the growth of public involvement in the UK economy during the first three-quarters of the twentieth century was seen as a consequence mainly of the development of parliamentary democracy and the attainment of universal adult franchise. The extension of voting power throughout the population meant that governments became more ready to facilitate the enactment of new legislation to regulate or constrain the activities of industry and commerce. The world of *laissez-faire*, if it had ever existed in any pure form, certainly receded from view, and business entrepreneurs found that they had to pay more attention to legal requirements, and that their environment was increasingly influenced by the decisions of public authorities. In a mixed economy, no successful businessman enjoys the luxury of being able to run his business exactly in accordance with his own interests and ideas. He must pay heed to the political and social forces constraining his activities.

This means first that the manager needs to be well aware of the state of the law concerning all aspects of his business. He needs to be up to date with the latest legislation which might affect his activities in any way, whether it is primary legislation enacted by Parliament, secondary legislation ordered by government ministers, or policy decisions by local and other public authorities. He needs to be aware of the pressures being brought to bear on all these decision-makers, not only so that he is not taken by surprise when decisions are made and new regulations enforced, but also so that his business's interests may also be represented, either directly or through a trade association, in the decision-making process.

The business world is made up of people who have the same rights as anyone else in the British system of parliamentary democracy to make their views known and to bring influence to bear on the political processes which produce new laws or decisions. Everyone with a stake in a business, as owner, manager, employee, customer or supplier, has the same democratic rights as any other members of the community, and it would be foolish not to exercise those rights and be involved in the political processes which lead to so many decisions affecting the operations of the business. The skilful business manager today needs to be alert to the political dimension of his company's interests; he needs to be able to initiate action in the political field to further those interests as far as possible within the constraints imposed by other social and political factors. He needs to be politically aware in relation to all the public bodies which can make decisions affecting the operations of his business.

Political systems differ from country to country, and inevitably this chapter concentrates on the system of parliamentary democracy applying within the UK, with the Westminster model of a bicameral parliament, in which the lower house is elected at least once every five years by universal adult suffrage, and with a system of local government set up and developed over the years in accordance with statute. Other countries, particularly within the Commonwealth, have parliamentary systems derived from the Westminster model, and it may be that many of the considerations within this chapter can be applied there, taking care to account for any differences of detail or emphasis. The next two sections, which describe the structure of national government and Parliament in the UK, will therefore include many points of relevance for business operators in other countries. The section after that concentrates more fully on the British scene, dealing with the more practical aspects of how British business managers may most effectively make representations to public bodies. Finally, since 1973 the UK has been a full member of the European Community (EC), and businesses in the UK are increasingly subject to the decisions of the institutions of the EC, so it is appropriate that the final section of this chapter should consider the European dimension in the relationship between management and government.

In all these ways, the political environment of a business is constantly changing, and the successful manager needs considerable knowledge to understand how present political structures have come about, how political decisions are being reached, and how future political factors may develop.

THE STRUCTURE OF NATIONAL GOVERNMENT IN THE UNITED KINGDOM

Before considering the British structure of government, it is important to note that the government and Parliament are two distinct, separate entities, although there are links and overlaps between them as described later. The basic distinction is that Her Majesty's Government, as the name implies, is appointed by the monarch on the advice of the prime minister and is responsible for the ongoing, executive administration of public service. Parliament, on the other hand, consists of two Houses, one of which, the House of Commons, is elected at least once every five years by universal adult suffrage. In the UK only Parliament can make primary legislation or statute law, much of which assigns powers or duties to members of the government, and only Parliament provides a representative forum for discussion of all issues affecting the life of the nation. Whereas in other countries, notably the United States, the executive and legislative bodies are kept deliberately and strictly apart, with only the Vice-President belonging to both, in the UK the pattern has developed whereby it is a rare exception for there to be a minister of the Crown who is not a member of one or other House of Parliament. (It so happens that there is such an exception at the present time, in the person of Mr Thomas Dawson QC, the Solicitor-General for Scotland.) But this overlap between the personnel of government and Parliament should not be allowed to cloud the distinction between the roles of the two bodies, of how they are formed in different ways, and of how either one may change while the other remains the same.

Her Majesty's Government consists simply of a relatively small number of men and women, at present 109, who are Her Majesty's Ministers, eighty-seven Members of the House of Commons, twenty-one Peers of the House of Lords and one Minister outside Parliament. They are all appointed formally by the Crown, although in practical terms the selection of ministers is made on the recommendation of the prime minister charged by the monarch to form a government. The structure of the government as a whole is shown in Figure 2, where the numbers indicate how many ministers there are in each category at the time of writing, June 1992; while these numbers have varied slightly from government to government, there have not been marked differences since the formation of the Northern Ireland Department in 1972. Three members of the government, all of them members of the House of Lords, are not accounted for in Figure 2 because they hold offices which are mainly ceremonial or relate to the Royal Household, like the Lord Chamberlain. The overall size of a government is limited by legislative provisions which restrict the number of persons who may draw salaries as ministers, and there is also a statutory requirement that a certain number of ministers must belong to the House of Lords, thereby ensuring that departments of the government are adequately represented in that chamber.

The structure of government shown in Figure 2 reveals four basic tiers of ministers. There is one head of the Government, generally known as the prime minister, whose official titles are First Lord of the Treasury and Minister for the Civil Service, and who is in effect appointed by the monarch of the day. The monarch does this whenever the office of prime minister becomes vacant, and the choice of new prime minister is generally guided by precedent or by the advice of former prime ministers, including, if possible, the one who has just left office. On most occasions in recent history, there has been an obvious person for the monarch to invite to

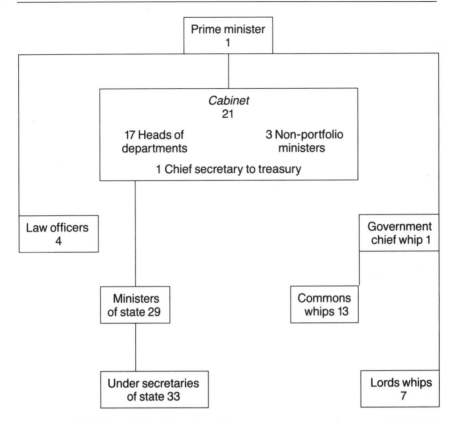

Of the 109 members of the government formed by John Major in April 1992, twenty-one were members of the House of Lords, eighty-seven members of the House of Commons, and one outside Parliament.

Figure 2 The structure of Her Majesty's Government

form a government, either because the prime minister has resigned and the government party has elected a new party leader, as in the case of Mr Callaghan in 1976 and Mr Major in 1990, or because the government party has been defeated at a general election, won with a clear majority by another party with a leader in position, as in the case of Mr Heath in 1970 or Mrs Thatcher in 1979.

On no occasion, however, in modern times has the monarch taken the initiative in inviting a person to be prime minister until the previous incumbent has tendered his or her resignation. So it was, for instance, after the general election of December 1923, when the Conservative government in which Mr Baldwin was prime minister lost its overall majority while remaining the largest party in the new House of Commons, that Mr Baldwin decided not to resign immediately. Instead he instructed ministers to prepare their proposals for inclusion in the King's Speech to be submitted to the new Parliament when it met in January 1924. It was only when the vote at the end of the debate on that speech in the House of Commons went against the government that Mr Baldwin then submitted the resignation of his government to King George V, and only then did the King invite the leader of the next largest party in the Commons, Mr MacDonald of the Labour Party, to form a government. Although Labour was in a considerable minority in the Commons, it was generally understood that the King wished this first Labour government to have a fair chance to govern and that he would be unwilling to grant a request for a further dissolution of Parliament within six months. As events turned out, that Parliament lasted only until October 1924, and in the following general election the Conservatives were returned with a large overall majority.

It is when a parliamentary situation arises without a clear, united party majority that the discretion of the monarch most comes into play with regard to the choice of prime minister. The one occasion this century when that happened was in December 1916, when the wartime coalition government in which Mr Asquith was prime minister fell. It then took George V some two days to find a successor, Mr Lloyd George, the process including a conference of the leaders of the different parties at Buckingham Palace. Furthermore, as we have noted in the events of 1924, the monarch does have some discretion in deciding whether to grant a prime minister's request for an early dissolution of Parliament. On one other occasion this century, it is possible that the views of the monarch led to a request for an early dissolution being made: in 1950 the general election had returned a parliamentary majority of only six for the Labour Party, and the prospect of political instability wore on into 1951, troubling the King, George VI, whose health was already giving grounds for concern and who may have wished to take action to ensure that the parliamentary scene was more settled in the event of his daughter coming to the throne. It was generally unexpected when the prime minister, Mr Attlee, sought a dissolution of Parliament in September 1951, but his request was granted, and the general election the following month produced a Conservative majority of seventeen. Mr Churchill then became prime minister, and was in office when Elizabeth II came to the throne in February 1952.

Having seen briefly how British prime ministers come into office, what powers do they exercise within government? The simple answer to that question is twofold. First, the constitutional arrangements in the UK give the incumbent prime minister the sole right to request the monarch to dissolve Parliament and issue a proclamation for the election of a new Parliament. The Parliament Acts require that no Parliament exists for more than five years from the day on which it first meets, but the monarch is able to dissolve any Parliament at an earlier date if the prime minister so requests; it was noted earlier that such a request is usually granted. Consequently the prime minister possesses the considerable power of being able to choose the date of the next general election, which power he will of course use to the advantage of his own political party; this power diminishes as the five-year limit for the life of a Parliament approaches. In addition, the power to recommend a dissolution of Parliament can strengthen the hand of a prime minister among his own ministerial colleagues and party members. If they are proving rebellious or are trying to undermine the prime minister's own position, the mere threat of a general election can be very effective in bringing them into line, especially if the government party is not doing well in opinion polls and some of them might lose their seats. Of course such tactics risk leading to the fall of the whole government and to the prime minister's own undoing, but that need not prevent the tactic being used as political bluff and brinkmanship.

The second function of the prime minister is to recommend the appointment of all other ministers of the Crown and to require their individual resignations when considered necessary. It is not easy to recall any instance in modern times of a minister refusing to resign when requested to do so by the prime minister, but presumably in such circumstances the minister would then be promptly dismissed by the monarch at the request of the prime minister. In effect, therefore, the prime minister has the power to 'hire and fire' all other ministers, and this gives him or her considerable influence over the conduct of all members of the government. In addition, it has to be noted that, when a prime minister resigns, the whole government is regarded as having resigned *en bloc*, and every portfolio is at the disposal of the monarch on the recommendation of the next prime minister. Consequently any minister who cannot be sure of office under another prime minister has a strong vested interest in the current prime minister's remaining in power.

Apart from these two basic functions, the prime minister's responsibilities are mainly related to security matters, to royal commissions or to ceremonial functions. Otherwise, nearly all the powers and duties of government are assigned to specific members of the government, and in the overwhelming majority of instances there is always a lower-ranked minister to whom any particular problem may be referred. Where some power has been granted to government by legislation, the wording of the enactment will usually specify which secretary of state or minister is to exercise that power. For instance the duty of government to pay retirement pensions to qualifying citizens of retirement age is expressed in the wording, 'the secretary of state shall pay', the reference there being to the Secretary of State for Social Security; and curiously there is no indication in any legislation as to how this payment should be made. Certainly in this instance, and in relation to most of the particular responsibilities of government, no duty is laid on the prime minister.

Similarly, historic precedent has assigned many particular responsibilities of government to the holders of offices of state other than the prime minister. For instance the Secretary of State for the Home Department, to give the Home Secretary his full title, has the historic right to be present at the actual birth of any royal baby who will be close in line to the throne. This curious right derives from the episode in July 1688, when a male heir was claimed as born to the Catholic King and Queen when only Catholics had been present; the prospect of a continuing line of Catholic monarchs led Protestants to allege that the baby had been smuggled into the queen's bedroom in a warming-pan, and the provision that future royal births be attended by the home secretary was consequently introduced. While today it is not the practice of home secretaries to exercise this right, they are still the first outside the royal family to be informed of any royal birth, and sometimes this requirement may delay the public announcement of the birth! There is no corresponding formal favour for the prime minister.

These examples demonstrate a more general principle relating to the distribution of responsibilities within government, namely that most ministers have particular jobs to perform and their portfolios are defined by custom and by statute. Consequently, when any citizen or group of citizens wishes to make representations to government to secure a change of policy or the introduction of some new measure, then those representations need to be made to the particular minister responsible for the area in question. Many people think that the clever thing to do is to go straight 'to the top' and contact the prime minister about their problems, but such a course is generally both vain and wasteful of time. Far more sensible is to ascertain beforehand the name and address of the responsible minister and to contact him or her directly.

It is therefore important to be conversant with the names of ministers who are currently holding the posts in the various ranks of government outlined in Figure 2. The full list of names of government ministers and the posts which they hold is given from time to time in leading daily newspapers, and appears at the front of every bound weekly edition of *Hansard*, the record of all that is said and transacted in the House of Commons. A fuller 'List of Ministerial Responsibilities', giving details of the specific portfolios of all ministers, is published from time to time by the management and personnel office within the government.

The second rank of government is essentially made up of the members of the Cabinet other than the prime minister. The size of the Cabinet has varied in modern times between twenty and twenty-three, most of whom are the heads of the various departments of government, from the Chancellor of the Exchequer, who in practical terms heads the Treasury, to the

Minister for Agriculture, Fisheries and Food. During recent years it has become the practice for a second Treasury minister, the Chief Secretary to the Treasury, also to have a seat in the Cabinet. In addition, the Cabinet includes three or four non-portfolio ministers, such as the Chancellor of the Duchy of Lancaster, the Lord President of the Council, or the Paymaster-General. These offices do have some historic or other administrative roles within government, but they are not in themselves supported by substantial departments of civil servants implementing large areas of public policy. Usually, these non-portfolio offices are used to provide seats in the Cabinet for the Leaders of the two Houses of Parliament, the political figures who steer the government's programme through Parliament, for ministers who have been assigned special areas of policy by the prime minister, usually overlapping several departments, or, when some Conservative governments have been in office, for the chairman of the Conservative Party. At present the party chairman, Sir Norman Fowler, happens to be a back-bench Conservative MP outside the government.

Within each of the seventeen main departments of government, ministers are arranged in three ranks. The head of the department is the relevant Cabinet minister, usually now with the title 'Secretary of State', although the Chancellor of the Exchequer, the Lord Chancellor and the Minister of Agriculture, Fisheries and Food are exceptions to this. Under the head of the department are a number of other ministers, ranging at present from one in the Lord Chancellor's Department to seven in the Department of the Environment. Some of them are Ministers of State, who for reasons of personal seniority or because of the importance of their responsibilities are regarded as the second rank of ministers, and the others are Under-Secretaries of State or Parliamentary Secretaries, the third rank. Some of these ministers are members of the House of Commons, others are Peers or Peeresses, spread through the government to enable an easy distribution of government spokesmen or spokeswomen in the House of Lords. All the main departments of government include at least one minister in the House of Commons. And in each department, the list of ministerial responsibilities is divided up between the various ministers, for ease of day-to-day administration, although very often the head of department will have no particular responsibilities in this way except oversight of all that is covered by the department. These divisions of the departmental portfolios are detailed in the 'List of Ministerial Responsibilities' mentioned earlier. When any citizen, engaged in business or elsewhere, wishes to make representations direct to government on any particular issue, the person to contact is therefore the minister whose listed portfolio includes the subject in question.

Other, non-departmental ministers are mentioned in Figure 2. They included the four law officers, two for England and Wales and two for Scotland. The former pair are the Attorney-General and the Solicitor-

General, who in addition to having important functions in the legal system, including at times acting as prosecuting counsel, are also charged with the general responsibility of providing legal advice to all other government ministers and departments. In Scotland, the Lord Advocate and the Solicitor-General for Scotland play corresponding roles within the different Scottish legal system. The main reason why the present Solicitor-General for Scotland is not a Member of Parliament is because only eleven of the seventy-two Scottish parliamentary seats are currently held by Conservatives and the prime minister has limited choice in filling the law offices from their ranks. The Lord Advocate, however, is a member of the House of Lords, and can therefore answer in that chamber on all Scottish legal matters, while the ministers of the Scottish Office are able to do the same in the House of Commons.

Finally there are at present twenty-one members of the government who are parliamentary whips. The government Chief Whip, whose official title is Parliamentary Secretary to the Treasury, has the prime responsibility of ensuring that all measures proposed by the government to Parliament will command a parliamentary majority there. He is present at all meetings of the Cabinet, although without a vote on the rare occasions when votes may be taken, and it is his duty to advise the Cabinet if he believes that any items for the government's parliamentary programme are unlikely to command a majority there. He is supported by a team of thirteen government whips in the House of Commons, most of whom have responsibilities on a regional basis for keeping in close touch with MPs of the government with constituencies in specific geographical regions. Overall it is the whips' role to ensure that there is always a majority to see that the government's programme proceeds smoothly through the Commons. There are seven more government whips in the House of Lords to perform a similar function in that chamber.

The UK pattern of government is essentially Cabinet government, in which all major decisions on government policy are reached by the Cabinet as a whole, if possible by consensus and on rare occasions by a majority vote. The doctrine of collective responsibility means that all members of the Cabinet, and indeed all other ministers as well, are publicly expected to defend the decisions of the Cabinet. There have been rare exceptions to this, when Cabinets have agreed publicly to disagree among themselves, for instance over imperial preferential tariffs during the coalition government of 1931–5, or over UK entry to the European Community in the run-up to the nationwide referendum of 1975. Within the Cabinet the prime minister is *primus inter pares*, a leader without being dominant, a chairman to hear and weigh the voices rather than to lay down the government line. Of course the personalities of different prime ministers lead them to different styles of Cabinet chairmanship. Of such material the whole interest in the UK system of government is built.

Before leaving this description of the structure of British government, it is useful to note that sponsored public bodies like the Manpower Services Commission or the Health and Safety Executive, mentioned in the previous chapter, are responsible to specific members of the government. In the cases of the two organizations just named, the sponsoring minister is the Secretary of State for Employment. So although these public bodies are not technically part of any government department, there is a large measure of ministerial responsibility for their operations, and there are appropriate ministers to receive representations on matters relating to them.

The links between government and Parliament

If members of the government are appointed by the monarch on the recommendation of the prime minister, and if the prime minister in turn is invited to form a government by the monarch, it is difficult to see at first how the UK system of government can be regarded as democratic. The element of democracy comes in fact from the requirement that the government is accountable to Parliament, on which it depends for the supply of finance from the public revenue for the maintenance of government. In Parliament the House of Commons is elected by a system of universal adult suffrage, regarded variously as being more or less democratic. It was the need for money which first led monarchs to call Parliaments, and in the Magna Carta of 1215 the barons insisted on the principle of 'no taxation without representation'; in other words they refused to pay taxes to support the king's government and his military campaigns unless they had some say in how much money was to be raised, how it was to be raised, and how it was to be used. The primary role of Parliament is to exercise some control on behalf of taxpayers over public expenditure, and through the centuries that control has come to be exercised more democratically, with the widening of the franchise for election of the House of Commons, and with the supremacy gained by that House over the Lords within Parliament. The extent of democratic control of government in the UK therefore depends on the effectiveness of the accountability of government to Parliament; we now turn to consider the ways in which this accountability operates.

In the first place, it is a general principle in the modern UK constitution that all ministers are members of one or other House of Parliament. Although there is currently an exception to this rule, the office involved is not central to government policy, and it is hardly likely that other more important exceptions would be allowed to persist. For instance, after the general election of 1964, when a Labour government came to office but the shadow foreign secretary, Patrick Gordon Walker, had lost his seat at Smethwick, the prime minister nevertheless advised the Queen to appoint

Mr Walker as foreign secretary, and a Labour back-bencher was persuaded to resign his seat at Leyton so that Mr Walker could contest the by-election in an attempt to return to Parliament. Throughout the period of the by-election Mr Walker remained the foreign secretary, and much of the nation's conduct of foreign affairs was directed from Leyton Town Hall. Unfortunately for Mr Walker, the people of Leyton did not take kindly to having him foisted upon them, and they elected another candidate to the Commons. Immediately, Mr Walker resigned as foreign secretary, as it was acknowledged that he could no longer continue in that office without being in Parliament. (He did, however, regain the Leyton seat at the general election in 1966, and subsequently returned to government and to membership of the Cabinet.)

It is generally required that ministers should be members of one of the Houses of Parliament in order that they are accessible to the other peers and representatives of the public, and in particular can be questioned on their conduct of public business. This contrasts with the situation in the United States, where the constitution strictly forbids any member of the administration from having a seat in Congress at the same time, apart from the Vice-President, who is ex officio the chairman of the Senate. During the period shortly before the American War of Independence it was felt that a similar 'division of the powers' would be necessary in the UK, because King George III had tried to pack Parliament with his own favourites whom he then appointed as ministers – 'the King's Friends'. During the following 150 years it became the practice for any newly-appointed minister with a seat in the House of Commons to be deemed to have vacated that seat upon appointment and then to contest the ensuing by-election, so that if again successful he could demonstrate that the public had confidence in him as their parliamentary representative, at the same time as holding an office of profit under the Crown.

This practice fell into disuse after 1921, following the remarkable case of Sir Arthur Griffith-Boscawen, who had been appointed Minister of Agriculture and Fisheries in the coalition government in which the prime minister was Mr Lloyd George. Sir Arthur, who was the Conservative MP for Dudley, then contested the consequent by-election on 3 March 1921, losing to Labour by seventy-six votes. He did not resign as minister there and then, but was returned to Parliament in another by-election at Taunton the following month. In the next general election, in November 1922, Griffith-Boscawen lost the Taunton seat to the Liberals, but the new prime minister, Mr Bonar Law, kept him in the Cabinet as Minister of Health. He therefore needed to find a parliamentary seat, and when a casual vacancy occurred in the formerly Conservative seat at Mitcham in Surrey he contested the by-election on 3 March 1923, but lost to the Labour candidate. So ended the ministerial career of Sir Arthur Griffith-Boscawen! And with him there ended, with general consent, the practice of requiring newly appointed ministers to resign their seats and contest the ensuing by-elections. All the same, most other offices of profit under the Crown are still regarded as incompatible with membership of the House of Commons; for instance High Court judgeships. Indeed, the accepted means of relinquishing membership of the Commons is to apply for the Stewardship of the Chiltern Hundreds or of the Manor of Northstead, at Scarborough, both crown appointments.

With these exceptions and historic provisos, it is accepted that membership of Parliament is a requirement for ministerial office, and this contributes one practical link in ensuring the democratic accountability of government. Those ministers who are members of the House of Commons all represent constituencies in the same way as other members there, and are therefore subject to democratic pressure from their electors and must seek re-election at each general election if they wish to continue in the Commons.

The presence of ministers within Parliament means that they are available there to give account of their stewardship in government, to speak in debates, to make ministerial statements and to give answers to parliamentary questions. These procedures all provide further means of ensuring the democratic accountability of government. Both in general debates and in the various stages of consideration of proposed new legislation, it is possible for ministers to be challenged and cross-examined on most aspects of government policy by any other members of Parliament, both in the Lords and in the Commons. These opportunities to challenge ministers in Parliament are of course taken up with considerable relish, and sometimes hostility, by opposition politicians. It is a recognized aspect of the British political system that the opposition has a duty to oppose the government; for that reason it is officially designated as Her Majesty's Opposition, and the Leader of the Opposition receives an official salary.

The effectiveness of this accountability of ministers through debates and questions in Parliament is limited by the fact that in these procedures ministers always have the last word, and there is no requirement in standing orders that the last word of a minister should provide a full, let alone relevant, answer to the question raised. So at question time in the House of Commons, oral questions are usually tabled up to a fortnight in advance, and ministers have ample time to be briefed by civil servants in preparing answers to them and to all the supplementary questions which they think may possibly arise. Such supplementary questions may be put by the MP who has asked the original question and then, at the discretion of the Speaker, who is usually in the chair at question time, by other members who are seeking to put questions, generally on the basis of questions being taken alternately from opposite sides of the chamber. No notice is required for supplementary questions, although each one needs to relate to the subject-matter of the original question, so it is possible for ingenious backbenchers or opposition spokesmen to pose unexpected supplementary questions which may well embarrass ministers. But a minister always has the right to reply after every such supplementary question, and he alone is responsible for the content of his reply; the Speaker has no power to intervene to force a minister to answer the point of any question. The same applies to supplementary questions which are always allowed after any ministerial statement. Members of Parliament have plenty of opportunities for airing issues and possibly embarrassing ministers, but little opportunity for forcing a minister to change some aspect of policy against his will.

Sometimes in the passage of a government bill through Parliament, the minister in charge of the bill may be willing to accept an amendment put by a member who is not in the government, and sometimes he will undertake to reconsider part of a bill in the light of the debate, with the possibility of bringing a government amendment at a later stage in the consideration of the bill. It is these circumstances which provide parliamentarians with their best opportunities of influencing government policy, and outside organizations and members of the public with further occasion to lobby ministers and other Members of Parliament.

Other times when there is good opportunity of influencing public policy through parliamentary lobbying include the days allocated for consideration of private members' bills, i.e. legislative proposals brought forward by back benchers rather than by ministers. Sometimes these proposals command all-party support, and if they are well forward in the queue for private members' bills they have a fair chance of reaching the statute book. On other occasions they may be very controversial, in which case sustained lobbying may effectively block their passage, as was the case with proposals to reform the law on Sunday trading early in 1983. That occasion provided a very real opportunity for business interests to make representations to Members of Parliament, both for and against the bill.

The oldest link between government and Parliament, as noted earlier, is the fact that Parliament approves the supply of funds from the public revenue for the maintenance of government. No government could continue in office for long without that supply or without approval for its overall budget and expenditure proposals in the form of finance bills, consolidated fund bills and appropriation bills. Consideration of all these measures gives parliamentarians an opportunity to comment on the expenditure programme of the government. When a government does not possess a working majority in the House of Commons, the votes on all these measures may be very close, and the loss of any such vote may be regarded as an indication that the government no longer has the confidence of the House. Similarly, the division in the Commons at the end of the debate on the Queen's (or King's) Speech is always regarded as a vote of confidence in the government; we have seen how the loss of such a vote led to the resignation of Mr Baldwin's government in January 1924. More generally, to lose the vote at the end of a censure debate, when the motion before the House is 'That this house has no confidence in Her Majesty's Government', is tantamount to a government's loss of the support of Parliament. The prime minister then has the choice of resigning or of recommending the dissolution of Parliament and the holding of a general election. Censure votes have been lost by governments twice this century, at the end of September 1924 and on 28 March 1979 (by a single vote). On both occasions general elections followed soon afterwards, at which the main opposition parties were returned victorious. It is at such times that the basic dependence of governments on Parliament is emphasized and the reality of parliamentary democracy experienced.

In less dramatic fashion, parliamentary scrutiny of the government's spending continues throughout the lifetime of a Parliament by means of the select committees. The oldest of these is the Public Accounts Committee (PAC) which systematically scrutinizes the accounts of all government departments after spending has taken place. The chairman of the PAC is always a senior opposition back-bencher, and the civil servant who has the main responsibility of presenting public accounts to the committee is the Comptroller and Auditor General, while the committee may also call for evidence from the accounting officers in all departments. Although the work of the PAC is undoubtedly very thorough and may reveal all manner of embarrassing discrepancies in government expenditure, the committee is unable to challenge the basic policies of government which underlie that expenditure. Furthermore, investigations by the committee take place after spending has occurred – often a considerable time after – so that any revelations are rather like shutting the stable door after the horse has bolted.

More constructive are the roles of the fourteen departmentally related select committees of the House of Commons which succeeded the former Expenditure Committee in 1979. Each of these committees consists of nine or eleven back-bench MPs, appointed by the full House of Commons after consultations between the various party whips, with representation on the committee broadly in proportion to the strengths of the parties in the House as a whole. The chairmanships of these committees are also apportioned according to the balance of parties in the House, so that at any time there are several chairmen from the opposition benches. Each committee has the power to investigate subjects of its own choosing within the whole field of the policy of the government department to which it relates, and in exercising this power it has absolute authority to send for relevant papers and persons and to travel anywhere in the UK collecting evidence. The effectiveness of these select committees varies according to their choice of subjects to investigate; in general they have more impact on government policy when tackling topical subjects which are outside the main field of party politics and where they may achieve a fair measure of cross-party unanimity. It is possible for select committee inquiries to influence the development of government policy as they proceed, and in any case reports issued by select committees may well be debated by the House as a whole and are always the subject of written official replies from the relevant government departments.

From the point of view of the business world, the opportunity of giving evidence to a select committee or of influencing the choice of a committee's topic of inquiry represents one of the more constructive openings for influencing public policy. Business companies or individual business managers who wish to air grievances over some aspect of government policy and who have proposals which they wish to see implemented by government do well to consider whether there is early opportunity for the particular subject to be investigated by a select committee. If so, an approach to the committee may be made by writing direct to the chairman or the clerk of the committee at the House of Commons. Such an approach would carry more weight if made through a trade association or through other sympathetic MPs. In any case, when a select committee decides on a topic to investigate, it will invariably make a public announcement to that effect and invite written evidence to be submitted by any interested parties. Whenever the topic is of importance to the interests of a business, it would be foolish for the business not to take up that opportunity, possibly in collaboration with others, and such written evidence may lead to an invitation from the committee to supplement it orally.

Another select committee of the Commons is the committee overseeing the work of the Parliamentary Commissioner for Administration (PCA), more popularly known as the Ombudsman. His office was set up by Act of Parliament in 1967 and his duties are simply to investigate complaints of maladministration by government departments. This remit includes anything that could be described as an administrative mistake, such as the mislaying of papers or the sending of a communication to an incorrect address, and in practice it has also been extended to include inconsistencies and unfairnesses in the application of a common overall policy. But in no way may the PCA investigate complaints about government policy itself. Furthermore, he is not able to receive complaints directly from members of the public or from organizations, but only through MPs, the principle being that those members are themselves the public representatives in all matters pertaining to government and as such may wish to conduct their own inquiries into a complaint before seeking the help of the PCA. But the PCA does have more extensive powers than an MP to help him in the investigation of a complaint, because he has the right of access to any department, to look through files for himself. The field of public administration where the PCA may investigate complaints ranges more widely than simply the formal departments of government, and includes most of the sponsored bodies reporting to government. The PCA is required by legislation to give an annual report on his work to the select committee.

Making representations about local matters

From time to time, a small business company or the manager of the local branch of a business may wish to raise with a public authority a particular problem concerned with the authority's policies or services. Care needs to be taken so that such a representation has the best chance of leading to a successful conclusion.

The first important step is to consider which authority has responsibility for the problem in question and the power to take steps to put the matter right in the way desired. Identification of the relevant authority is not always straightforward; many inquiries about problems 'go off at half-cock' because the wrong authority is approached in the first instance. The most common mistake in this respect, in almost all parts of the community, including the business world, is to confuse national government with local government. Many people who are concerned about some issue which may lie wholly within the jurisdiction of a local authority act under the illusion that their case will have a better chance of success if they refer it in the first instance to a parliamentary representative or to a government minister. Even though the British public generally claim to be staunch supporters of local democracy, many people still think that the man in Whitehall or Westminster has more political 'clout' and is able to tell local authorities what to do. While this approach may be successful on odd occasions, it may also be disastrous, for local authorities can be jealous of their independence and resent interference from above, especially if that interference is via a political agency of a different political colour from the local council. In any case, local democracy is undermined by any attempt to by-pass the local channels which exist direct to a local authority or via the locally elected councillors.

So it helps in making representations about local matters to know what subjects are entirely the responsibility of local authorities. The scene in this respect is further confused by the fact that, whereas in Greater London and in the metropolitan counties of England there is only one tier of local government, in the non-metropolitan counties there are at present two tiers, namely county and district councils, while in Scotland there are regional and district councils. Wherever there are two tiers of local government, it is important to know the division of responsibility between the two. Suffice to say here that, while all district councils are responsible for public housing provision, for public health and refuse collection, for recreational amenities and for local planning matters, in the non-metropolitan counties the county council is the local educational authority, the local highway authority and has responsibility for all social services, for police and fire services, for libraries and museums and for strategic planning matters. Where there is only one tier of local authority, all functions of local government are of course the responsibility of that authority or of joint committees of several adjacent authorities.

The picture is further complicated because there are several 'grey' areas in the division of responsibility between local and national government in the UK. For instance, when an application is made for planning permission for some new development, that application is generally considered in the first instance by the local planning authority, the district council. If that authority grants the application, the matter is settled. However, if the local authority declines the application, or grants it subject to conditions, then the applicant has the right of appeal to the Secretary of State for the Environment either against the refusal of planning permission or against one or more of the conditions. If such an appeal is made, the matter moves from the sphere of local government to the national level. Similarly, in the field of education, any proposals to cease to maintain a school in the local authority system must be made in the first instance by the relevant local education authority, but then representations may be made against the proposals by ten or more local government electors to the Secretary of State for Education.

When it has been carefully established which is the relevant authority for dealing with any particular problem, representations should then be made to the democratically elected representative for that authority. If the matter correctly falls within the area of national government, then the appropriate elected representative will be a Member of Parliament for a local constituency. If the problem is one for a local authority, then the appropriate county councillor or a local district councillor should be approached. While there is no invariable method for making such an approach, in the case of parliamentary representatives the most suitable means of communication is by letter, the address for correspondence being at all times of the year 'House of Commons, London, SW1A OAA.' For local authority representatives, local circumstances will determine whether the best means of approach is by writing, by telephone or by personal meeting.

Whenever representations are made by business interests to Members of Parliament, it is always wise to emphasize how the issues involved affect the local community, even when they are issues of national significance. Any local MP will naturally take more notice of arguments which demonstrate how the interests of his own constituents are affected by the problem under discussion, particularly when there is some special effect locally. Therefore when a business association is mounting a national campaign of parliamentary representation on some question and contacts its members throughout the country, exhorting them to write to their local MPs, it is important to resist the temptation to forward documents which have been circulated by the association, or to copy those documents verbatim. It is easy for an MP to work out that such a letter to him is part of an orchestrated national campaign, and he is less likely to take an active interest in supporting that campaign unless he sees how it will particularly help his own constituents; after all, it is their interests that he is elected primarily to represent. The help of the MP is much more likely to be forthcoming if the approach to him is couched with special reference to local circumstances and if steps are taken to disguise the fact that the representations are part of a national campaign.

On many occasions it is thought useful to bring pressure to bear on democratically elected representatives by means of petitions with many signatures. In the business context the signatures might be those of employees or customers of a firm. However, while such petitions do provide an elected representative with clear evidence that the signatories have called for certain action to be taken – and such evidence can be useful later if the action is taken but then provokes protest – by and large, petitions do little to advance the cause which they advocate. Petitions have become devalued over the years; their basic weakness is that many people sign them because they are under pressure to do so, particularly if they are employees of the firm whose manager is organizing the petition. When signatures to a petition are sought by a doorstep campaign, many people will sign quickly in order to be rid of the caller and to get back to the television! Similarly, customers at a store may gladly put their signatures to some kind of petition if they think this is the quickest way of getting on with their shopping. In making public representations on any issue, the strength of reasoned argument is far more important than the number of signatures.

Finally, business managers who wish to lobby local representatives about some issue may be uncertain as to which representative to contact. With regard to MPs, for example, any individual citizen may usually say with precision who is his or her own MP, namely the member for the geographical constituency which includes the person's home address, and where the person's name appears on the electoral register. But the situation for business organizations is much less straightforward. Even if the business is located on only one site and it is easy to identify the parliamentary constituency which includes that site, there is no guarantee that any of the stakeholders connected with the business are constituents of the MP for that constituency. Indeed, the interests of residents living near the business site, who are of course constituents of the member in question, may be opposed to the interests of the business in respect of the matter to be raised; meanwhile the managers, employees and shareholders may live in other constituencies.

This uncertainty can often arise when the site of a business is in an urban, heavily populated area, where people's journeys to work cross several constituency boundaries, and where there may be a large number of MPs whose constituents include stakeholders of the business. In these circumstances, the local manager needs to do some research to see whether there is perhaps a group of a handful of MPs, say not more than six, whose constituents include the majority of the local workforce, to whom identical representations can be made. It can be particularly useful if that group of MPs includes members belonging to two or more different political parties, for representations will then be channelled across a wider political spectrum and hopefully bring pressure to bear from all sides. So, for example, if a firm is based on Merseyside, there is a useful opportunity at present for representations to be made via local MPs belonging to three different political parties.

INVOLVEMENT IN THE EUROPEAN COMMUNITY

On 1 January 1973 the United Kingdom became a member state of three separate communities, namely the European Economic Community (EEC), the European Coal and Steel Community and Euratom, which have since been linked together as the European Community (EC). The EEC had been in existence since the Rome Treaty of 1957, which six European states had signed: France, West Germany, Italy, Belgium, the Netherlands and Luxembourg. After various unsuccessful attempts in the 1960s for the UK to join the communities, this step came about following successful negotiations by the UK government headed by Mr Heath in 1971 and the passage through the UK Parliament of the European Communities Act in 1972. Denmark and Ireland also joined the EC at that time; more recent additions have been Spain, Portugal and Greece. The unification of Germany in 1990 added the former territory of East Germany to the EC, and an application for membership of the EC made by Austria in 1989 is currently under negotiation. Sweden and Finland have started the formal procedure to become full EC members by 1995, in Switzerland a public referendum is planned for December 1992 to determine whether that country should apply for EC membership, and changes in eastern Europe during the last two years have opened up many possibilities of widening the membership of the EC in that direction, with the Hungarian government now intending to seek EC membership.

The Treaty of Rome is a long document covering most aspects of the economic and commercial policies of member states of the EC. The primary objective of achieving abolition of customs barriers within the EC – and therefore common external tariffs – had largely been achieved by the six original member states by 1968, and has been extended to new members fairly quickly after their accession. Another fundamental area of the Treaty concerns the Common Agricultural Policy, with harmonization between member states of methods of agricultural support. The main structure of this had been determined before British accession. Similarly the outline of the Common Fisheries Policy was put together during the 1970s, as was the move to harmonization of methods of indirect taxation within member states, largely using value added tax.

The Treaty also provides for increasing harmonization on all taxation matters throughout the EC, but it is recognized that questions of taxation touch very sensitively on questions of national sovereignty, and the agencies of the EC have therefore followed a policy of proceeding slowly towards this end, taking such steps as were possible at any particular time. Progress has been more rapid in recent years towards achieving a Single European Market (SEM) by the end of 1992. The definition of this concept is 'an area without internal frontiers in which the freedom of movement of goods, services, capital and persons is ensured'. A key part of the programme to achieve SEM is the adoption of uniform technical standards to ensure that free competition between goods is on a fair basis, with different states mutually recognizing each others' products as being properly comparable with their own. By the beginning of 1991, 282 specific measures dealing with particular items for achieving SEM had been proposed by the Commission of the EC, and at that time over 200 of these had been agreed by the machinery of the EC itself, but only twenty-one had already been implemented by all member states. The speed of implementation of agreed EC proposals varies greatly from one member state to another, with Denmark having the best record, implementing over 80 per cent of such proposals to date. Another 800 sets of proposals on achieving harmonization of technical standards are still due to appear from the Commission. In the longer term, the Commission has set a target of achieving a single currency within the Community by 1999.

This brief survey of the scope of the EC shows how its decisions may have the most direct bearing on the operations of a business anywhere within the EC. Not only do businesses need to adjust in order to face more direct competition in their home market from other EC producers, but they need to expand their marketing and exporting activities to exploit the opportunities opening up in other markets within the EC. Furthermore, a very close watch needs to be kept on all proposals affecting technical standards, for these may have considerable bearing on the marketing of a company's products, or may necessitate changes in methods of production. A business therefore needs to develop the ability to lobby at the European level, and to do this it helps to have some knowledge about how decisions in the EC are reached.

There are broadly three centres of decision-making in the EC: namely the Council of Ministers, the Commission, and the Assembly. The Council of Ministers is made up of ministers from each of the governments of the member states of the EC; generally, each government will send to a particular meeting of the Council its own minister whose portfolio relates to the business to be conducted at the meeting. The chair at such a meeting is taken by the minister from the country which is currently holding the presidency of the Council, this office rotating around member states and being held for six months at a time. The Council discusses proposals brought to it by members of the Commission, who are the full-time executive officers of the EC, appointed by the governments of member states for four-yearly periods, there being two Commissioners from the larger states and one from each of the others. The portfolios of the Commissioners are determined by the Commission as a whole at the beginning of its period of office, and the presidency of the Commission rotates by nation on a four-yearly basis. The European Assembly, or Parliament, is composed of public representatives, directly elected since 1979 in accordance with electoral systems determined by member countries, who are able to debate proposals from the Commission and to put questions to Commissioners, and who have the considerable power of being able to withhold approval from the annual Community budget. While the European Assembly cannot take the initiative in making EC legislation, its role as a public watchdog is steadily growing more influential, and members of the Assembly have a ready entrée into most of the corridors of power of the EC.

Anyone with a problem connected with the decision-making processes of the EC, and that includes business managers just like any other citizens, may seek to bring influence to bear on those processes, either through ministers of the home government who attend the Council of Ministers, or through representatives in the European Assembly. While ministers may have more power in such matters, it may take time for them to be mobilized, and in any case they may not be so ready to agree with the point of view of the complainant. It is therefore wise in most instances to make a two-pronged approach in lobbying on such a matter: via a Westminster MP to enlist the active assistance of the relevant government minister, and via the Euro-MP for the local Euro-constituency. Because Euro-constituencies are much larger than Westminster constituencies, there being on average nine of the latter to each of the former, it may be relatively easy to determine which Euro-MP is the appropriate person to contact on any particular issue, although it may be more difficult to make actual contact with him or her. There is no doubt, however, that in the needs of business people to make public representations, the role of the local Euro-MP is of increasing visibility and usefulness. The power of the EC was demonstrated during 1991 by the first ruling of the European Court of Law that an item of UK statute law, namely the Merchant Shipping Act 1987, was invalidated by overriding considerations in the Treaties of the EC.

Chapter 4

Business and law

THE STRUCTURE OF THE COURTS SYSTEM IN ENGLAND AND WALES

In the previous chapter attention was given to the interaction between business management and the processes of public political decision-making. Many of the decisions of government and Parliament are enacted in the form of statute law, and are generally enforced through the courts of law. However, statute law is only one part of the legal system of the United Kingdom, much emphasis also being placed on case law established by precedent. All this legal framework for the community represents another area of interface between the world of business and society as a whole, and business managers need increasingly to be aware of the legal implications of their business activities, and of how their businesses may be involved in legal actions. So in this chapter we consider the current legal background for business, the system of courts and the cases they hear, the legal obligations of companies, and the practical methods for businesses to obtain legal advice and assistance.

It is important first to note that legal and judicial systems differ greatly from country to country, partly because of considerable political differences but equally because of different legal traditions. The system in England and Wales is based more on an adversarial approach between the parties in a case and relies strongly on case law, whereas on the mainland of Europe legal courts adopt a more investigatory approach, with a stronger reliance on codified law, based originally on the system of law of the Roman Empire.

For historical reasons, the Scottish legal system has a closer affinity with the European system than with the English system. It is crucial for UK companies to appreciate that there is an entirely different legal jurisdiction in Scotland compared with England and Wales, with different traditions and different laws, as well as a different structure of courts and different legal officials. Whereas the kingdoms of England and Scotland were united in 1603, and there has been a single Parliament for all of Great Britain since 1707, the original separate legal systems have continued in the two different jurisdictions, and very many enactments have to be made separately for Scotland. In this section the description of the system of courts therefore applies only to England and Wales (which we shall abbreviate as 'the English system'). The reader would need to look elsewhere for similar information on the legal systems in Scotland or in other countries.

One basic principle of the English system is the distinction between criminal trials, where the defendant is accused of an offence under the criminal law and the case is brought on behalf of the Crown by a prosecuting authority, and civil actions, where one private party is suing another for some alleged wrong action. These two different categories of case proceed differently through the courts' system, which is shown in diagram-

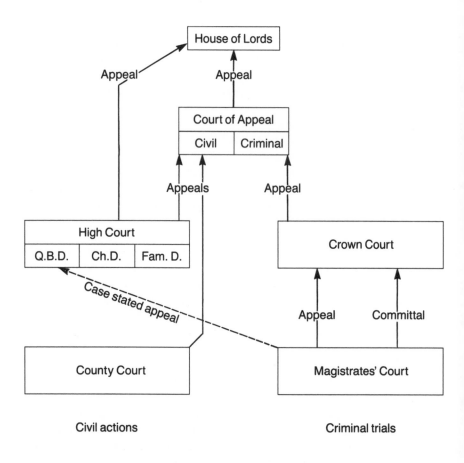

Figure 3 The courts system of England and Wales

matic form in Figure 3. In the first instance all criminal cases are heard in the magistrates' courts, by either three, or sometimes two, lay magistrates, or by a single stipendiary magistrate. The proceedings in criminal cases in a magistrates' court will hear some cases completely and reach convictions and, where defendants are found guilty, sentences. In other cases magistrates may simply hear committal proceedings for sending defendants to trial in a crown court, either because of the nature of the offence or because defendants elect for trial by crown court, where they will be heard by a jury of twelve independent, lay people. In any criminal case where a magistrates' court reaches a decision, the defendant has the right of appeal against that decision to the crown court, and similarly there is a right of appeal against decisions of a crown court to the criminal division of the Court of Appeal at the Old Bailey. It is now possible in some cases where a court has convicted a defendant, but the prosecution is dissatisfied with the level of sentence passed, for the prosecution to appeal to a higher court to increase the sentence.

Civil actions may begin either in county courts or in the High Court, which has three divisions: the family division for dealing with matrimonial and children's questions, the chancery division, presided over historically by the Lord Chancellor but nowadays by the Vice-Chancellor, for hearing cases generally on financial matters like probate or bankruptcy, and the Queen's Bench division for hearing all other civil cases. It is possible for some appeals in criminal cases heard in magistrates' courts to be taken to the Queen's Bench division of the High Court when they are 'case stated' appeals, based on legal technicalities. All defamation cases start in the High Court, where they may be heard by juries. Appeals arising from cases heard by the High Court usually go to the civil division of the Court of Appeal, in the Law Courts at the Strand in London, where they are heard by three appeal judges sitting together, or in some instances it may be possible to appeal directly from the High Court to the House of Lords, when in the general public interest there is urgent need for an authoritative ruling on some point of law. In any case heard by the Court of Appeal, in either the civil division or the criminal division, it is possible for dissatisfied parties to seek to appeal to the House of Lords, such leave to appeal being granted either by the Court of Appeal itself or by the House of Lords. Similarly, the House of Lords may hear appeals in civil actions from Scotland, but not in criminal cases from that jurisdiction.

Further explanation is necessary of the role played by the House of Lords in the legal system, as the final and highest court of appeal in the UK, beyond which there is no further appeal. Although the Lord Chancellor is both the head of the judiciary and presides over the whole House of Lords from the Woolsack, the legislative and judicial roles of the Lords are exercised entirely separately. The judicial role is the prerogative of the Law Lords, who at any one time are at most eleven senior judges, including some from Scotland, who are ennobled with life peerages precisely to fulfil this role under the leadership of the Lord Chancellor, who appoints them to hear particular appeals. Hearings are held, by three, five or seven Law Lords together, in a committee room at the end of the main committee corridor in the Palace of Westminster. It is interesting that, whereas judges in all lower courts wear wigs and gowns, the Law Lords are attired in lounge suits as they hear appeals. It is later when Law Lords deliver judgments from their special bench in the chamber of the House of Lords that they are fully robed and wigged. Law Lords may and do take part in all other proceedings of the House of Lords, normally without any special dress; when doing so they sit on the cross-benches of the chamber, neither supporting nor opposing the government.

Of course, seeking justice through the courts can be an expensive business, the basic principle being that the full costs of both sides are met by the unsuccessful party, in addition to any fines incurred or awards made. Even when an individual citizen is sure of his innocence or the rightness of his case, the possibility of having to meet huge legal costs at the end of the legal procedure may be a sufficient deterrent to stop him going to law. Similar financial considerations apply to businesses, although the larger funds at their disposal increases the opportunities for taking legal action, and business managers and directors may well consider the risk of legal costs as one worth taking if there are significant financial benefits to be gained by the company from a successful case. We now turn to consider the most likely ways in which a business in this country may find itself as a party in a legal action.

HOW A BUSINESS MAY BE INVOLVED IN LEGAL ACTION

It was noted in Chapter 2 that until 1844 business companies had no legal entity, and the only way for them to be involved in legal action was as partnerships of their individual shareholders. Consequently the same rules and procedures which applied to legal actions concerning individual citizens applied equally when companies sued or were sued. This was changed by the Registration Act 1844 and all the subsequent company legislation, under which it is possible for a company to be represented in court in its own name. For many years, however, it remained impossible for companies to be prosecuted in any criminal trials, and so their court appearances were entirely in civil cases. For instance, in 1929 the Glamorgan Assizes considered a case where a person had been electrocuted by an electric fence surrounding a coal tip, but ruled that the colliery company could not be guilty of manslaughter. This was because until 1948 the only penalties which courts were able to impose in criminal cases were either custodial sentences or the death sentence, neither of which could sensibly be applied when the defendant was a company. In the Magistrates Act

1948, however, fines were introduced for the courts to impose following most criminal cases, and it immediately became sensible for such fines to be levied against companies. Note, however, that this still means that companies cannot be sentenced for murder or treason, for neither of which financial penalties are available, and so it does not make sense for companies to be prosecuted for these criminal offences.

Apart from these two offences there is now no reason in principle why companies should not face prosecution for criminal offences in the UK, always of course depending on the merits of the case as to whether such charges should be brought by the prosecuting authorities or found proved by the courts. However, while charges of corporate manslaughter, for instance, have been very seriously considered in several recent instances, they have in general not proceeded or have been dropped in court because there was considered to be insufficient evidence available to convince the court of criminal guilt. This is partly because of the general principle in English law that a company is separate from the people belonging to it, and partly because many criminal charges required the proof of *mens rea*, i.e. deliberate intent before the criminal act on the part of the defendant. While companies can be held to be vicariously liable for crimes committed by their employees in the course of their employment, it does not follow automatically that the guilty mind of an employee is the guilty mind of the company as a whole. Such questions involve deep legal and even philosophical discussion (*vide* Davies and Holdcroft 1991) and will only rarely concern the practical business manager, but it does need to be remembered that under the law of England and Wales it is now possible for very serious criminal charges to be brought against companies.

More common, however, is the likelihood of a company being taken to a magistrates' court on a charge of infringement of pollution control or public health regulations, which are criminal matters with severe financial penalties. Recent court cases have also involved the prosecution of businesses for contravening the Sunday trading provisions of the Shops Act 1950. In all these examples the prosecuting authority will tend to be the relevant department of the local authority, rather than the crown prosecution service, but the hearings are criminal trials none the less.

Since 1844 the bulk of court hearings in which companies have been parties have been civil cases. Such actions may unfortunately arise in all the dealings that a company has with other companies or with individual customers or employees. Some of the simplest civil cases involve action to recover bad debts, and for amounts up to £5,000 the small claims procedure operated through the offices of county courts is relatively simple and inexpensive, not requiring legal representation. Other civil cases arise from breach of contract or failure to fulfil contract requirements, and if these cannot be resolved by private agreement through legal representatives they may lead to complicated court hearings. Other suits may be for negligence on the part of a business company, or for breach of patent of copyright. One area of civil litigation which may grow in future in the UK, as it has already done in other countries, relates to product liability, whereby a manufacturer or supplier may be held liable for damages arising from the particular nature of the product.

An increasing number of disputes involving business companies lead to hearings, not in the criminal or civil courts, but before industrial tribunals of one kind or another. Such tribunals are established by statute law and hear claims, usually from employees or their representatives, on subjects like unfair dismissal or compensation for industrial injury. While tribunals do not have the same level of authority or privilege as courts of law, their procedures are semi-judicial and broadly follow the same lines as court procedures. For some tribunals there is the opportunity of appeal against a tribunal decision to the High Court, although the grounds for such appeal are usually restricted to technical points of law. It is increasingly common for parties appearing before a tribunal to be legally represented, and the branch of the legal profession undertaking such work is expanding rapidly.

For many years after 1844 the scope for taking a company to court in civil actions was limited by the *ultra vires* rule. Briefly, this meant that a company as such was legally liable for matters arising only from the exercise of its powers and responsibilities as listed in its official memorandum of association. If the board of a company undertook some activity not covered by those powers and responsibilities, then the activity was technically *ultra vires* and the company could not be sued for any consequence of that activity. This of course did not stop legal action being taken against directors as individuals for the results of their *ultra vires* activity, or indeed shareholders taking action against their own directors for using company resources in ways that were *ultra vires*. However, the growth of many modern business companies, particularly with the diversification of their activities, has limited considerably the application of the *ultra vires* rule, and court judgments in particular cases have established precedents which cause doubt as to whether the rule now has any power in England and Wales.

From this very cursory introductory survey of how companies may be involved in legal action, it is clear that the field is one of extraordinary complexity, and in all but the simplest cases it is wise, although expensive, for professional legal representation to be hired. The following section therefore considers how best a business company in England and Wales today may go about securing professional legal advice and representation.

Companies and professional lawyers

In the great majority of instances in England and Wales where companies face criminal charges or are in legal dispute with other parties, it is normal – and indeed wise – for the company to obtain professional legal representation. While it is technically possible for a defendant in court to conduct his or her own defence, it is generally not wise to attempt to do so, because of the complexity of law and because of the procedural minutiae involved in many court hearings. The legal profession has two distinct branches, namely solicitors who are able to represent clients in all matters dealt with out of court and who may also appear in magistrates' courts, and barristers who appear in all other courts and provide expert advice in the form of counsels' opinions. Recent legal reforms have made it possible for solicitors to appear in higher courts in appropriate cases, but by and large the two branches of the profession are separate in function and in personnel.

Traditionally, companies which have become involved in some legal case or dispute have sought legal advice by first approaching a solicitor or firm of solicitors in the same way as any other individual client. There may have been some firm of solicitors with longstanding links with the company, whose services are regularly sought in all legal matters, or a solicitor may be approached because he has a good reputation for specializing in the branch of law covering the matter in question. As inquiries on the case proceed, the solicitor acting for the company may advise that counsel's advice be sought from a barrister, or that a barrister be engaged to prepare for the case to be taken to court. The choice of barrister is of course for the client to make, but it is unusual for the advice of the solicitors handling the case not to be heeded. That advice will be based on the reputations of barristers in handling cases in their specialist fields, and also on knowledge of what fee levels particular barristers can command. Not surprisingly, the services of more skilful barristers are in greater demand and can command higher fees. If a case is fairly open and shut and the outcome is unlikely to depend on the special skill of the barrister, then it would be a luxury to employ the services of an expensive advocate.

With the growing size of some companies, however, it has become increasingly common for them to have their own legal departments, the staff of which include qualified solicitors employed full-time by their firms. All legal problems and queries arising in the company's operations are then referred in the first instance to the legal department, either simply for advice or for action as appropriate. If solicitor's letters need to be sent to other parties, then these can be dealt with by a solicitor on the company's pay-roll, although in some specialized branches of the law it might still be thought wise to use a professional from an outside firm of solicitors. And certainly if the services of a barrister are required, either to provide counsel's opinion or to appear in court, then these will always have to be sought from outside the company, in the same way as if a private firm of solicitors were engaged.

It is therefore of interest to consider the arguments for and against whether a company should employ its own lawyers full-time, or whether it should always seek outside legal help. The first aspect to be considered here is bound to be financial, and a company needs to consider whether the cost of employing suitable legal staff will be more or less than the cost of using outside solicitors instead. One advantage to be gained by having in-house lawyers, especially if they have been employed for some years and are well-versed in the operations of the company, is that extra time and expense is not incurred in briefing outside lawyers to do the same work. Furthermore, whenever legal advice is needed inside a company in order for its policies to be framed correctly, it is relatively easy for that advice to be obtained in-house and without the cost disincentive which might deter the pursuit of outside advice. On the other hand, it is easier for outside lawyers to be totally objective in their advice and to tell a company something it may not wish to hear, whereas an internal lawyer would need to have courage in saying things which in some companies might jeopardize his own chances of advancement as an employee.

The longer that a lawyer is employed full-time by a company, the more he becomes specialized in all its affairs, and the more quickly he can respond with good legal advice and take appropriate legal action when the need arises. He will be able to follow legal developments specifically relating to the operations of the company, and he will know which barristers to employ when necessary to represent the company in court. Furthermore, with the growing internationalization of the activities of most large companies, particularly on the European scene, the in-house lawyer will have a better chance than an outsider of developing his own knowledge and experience of different legal jurisdictions, and will save his company from having to hire outside lawyers in every different jurisdiction on every issue that may arise.

In summary, as soon as the size of a company and of its legal requirements justifies employing an in-house solicitor, then on balance it is probably best to do so, especially if the firm operates in several countries, and the advent of the European Single Market gives an international flavour to most companies' marketing arrangements whether they like it or not. It is important for anyone seeking advice from an in-house lawyer to recognize, however, that good legal advice may not always coincide with what they would like to hear, so care must be taken not to undermine the objectivity of the in-house lawyer or to reduce his confidence that his prospects will not be affected by the popularity of the advice which he has to offer.

Chapter 5

Business and ethics

THE TOPICALITY OF BUSINESS ETHICS

In recent years interest has grown within business circles in the UK, the USA and other western economies in the improvement of ethical standards within business activity. This has come about partly because of consumer pressure, with customers being more ready to do business with firms which have a reputation for being 'ethical', particularly in their attitudes to environmental issues and matters of social responsibility. At the same time businesses have reacted to the widespread publicity given to a number of court cases on both sides of the Atlantic concerning charges of business malpractice, insider dealing, fraud and other criminal activity in business dealings. This publicity has brought to light an unacceptable face of the business world, which has therefore responded by giving more attention to ethical standards in business, either to improve the image of business cosmetically, or through a genuine concern to find better ways of conducting commercial activity. Contemporary managers therefore need to have a fuller understanding of 'business ethics', so this chapter is devoted to examining aspects of this particular boundary between management and the community at large.

The simple definition of the term 'business ethics' is that it is the application to business activity of ethics, the study of morals or principles of what is right or wrong in human behaviour. Exponents of business ethics attempt to establish what is proper conduct in the context of business, whether individual or corporate conduct. Historically and logically, however, it is possible to distinguish at least three different kinds of ethics, based respectively on three separate approaches to the question of what is right or wrong. Studying the writings of the major moral philosophers can lead to much intellectual confusion, unless it is perceived that there are these three different bases for developing ethical principles. Such confusion is then magnified when it is carried across to the application of ethics in any particular field of human activity, such as business and commerce.

Social ethics

The word 'ethics' is derived from the Greek *ethikos* and *ethos*, which relate to the 'prevalent tone or sentiment of a people or community' (*Shorter Oxford English Dictionary*). To the Greeks, ethics was a practical science in which the basic rules were founded on a recognition of what was generally accepted in society as 'good'. It was the *ethos*, or climate of opinion in a society, which determined the standards by which right or wrong conduct was to be judged. This kind of ethics was determined directly by the society to which the individual belonged, and it can therefore appropriately be described as 'social ethics'.

Of course the society which provided this framework for Socrates, Plato, Aristotle and the other Greek philosophers of the time was the Greek city-state, the *polis*, narrowly confined within its own city limits. And within that society the ethos was set by those who were Greek citizens, while the slaves or helots were ignored. So the standards of ethics were determined by a relatively small society, and the need for social acceptability was the prime incentive for ethical conduct. Different cities were capable of producing different ethical climates, especially when they were in conflict with one another, and ethical standards were generally lower in relations between people of different cities than between fellow-citizens. Furthermore, the treatment of slaves was guided by ethical standards only in so far as there were standards accepted by the main body of citizens, and not by consideration of the fact that slaves were part of the society which created the ethos. Similarly, social ethical standards had no application in relations between Greeks and non-Greeks, and no attempt was made to practise ethics in military operations against foreigners such as the Persians. From the time of Alexander the Great onwards, there were Greeks who realized the limitations of their ethical standards were not applicable to international relations, and who saw that social ethics had the weakness of not applying outside the home society.

The same was true of other ancient peoples. Although the tribes of Israel based their code of ethics, as described in the Pentateuch, on divine commandments, still most of them saw those ethics as applicable only within their own nation, and generally they did not practise the same ethical standards in their relations with Gentiles. The Romans, too, based their moral standards on the *mores*, or customs, of their own societies of citizens, so those standards did not relate in general to relations with slaves or foreigners. Yet as the Roman Empire expanded to cover most of the civilized world, taking in peoples of many races, religions and cultures, the weakness of social ethics was increasingly appreciated. Therefore, while Roman courts of law were available for settling disputes between Roman citizens, it was also recognized that there had to be 'a court for foreigners' to hear cases involving aliens, and special praetors were appointed, based in Rome but travelling throughout the provinces, to bring justice to peoples with different backgrounds and ethical standards, in accordance with *jus gentium*, the common law of nations.

Within nations and communities, however, the prevalence of social ethics continued, and remains strong even today. The French philosopher Montesquieu was able to see that different forms of society produced different patterns of ethics: he observed that the dominant ethos of despotism was fear, of monarchies honour, and of republics virtue (MacIntyre 1967: 179). While this simplistic classification may have reflected Montesquieu's own prejudices, he was correct to suggest that different forms of political structure produce very different moral climates and different standards of what is regarded as 'good'. Indeed, while high ethical standards may be observed within a society itself, social ethics often results in a citizen's acting outside that society, in its best interests, without any sense of right or wrong in what he is doing. The patriot will drink to Decatur's toast of 1816, 'Our country, right or wrong', (Mackenzie 1844: chap. xiv), and Dr Johnson was able in 1775 to observe that 'patriotism is the last refuge of the scoundrel' (Boswell 1791: vol. 2, 348). Very often the relationships between nations are not regarded as suitable areas for the practice of ethics; the former British Prime Minister, Mr Edward Heath, observed in a BBC radio broadcast in 1990 that it is not possible to conduct international relations on the basis of morality. Similarly, Karl Marx based his social ethics on the accepted standards within a social class, and could not see how the struggle between different classes could be conducted in accordance with any ethical principles. For Marx, 'in matters of conflict between social classes the appeal to moral judgements was not only pointless but positively misleading' (MacIntyre 1967: 213).

While the weakness of social ethics is that they break down in situations involving relations between different societies, their strength can be that they are relatively easy to define, and it is much easier to be identified with the interests of one's own society than with a set of abstract ethical principles. In the words of one of the characters in Ian Fleming's *Casino Royale*, advising the hero, 'Surround yourself with human beings, my dear James. They are easier to fight for than principles' (Fleming 1955: 147). Loyalty to one's family, or town, or political party, or class, or country can be a very easy and convenient substitute for any set of ethical standards in relationships outside the loyalty-group. And social ethics in general is really a sophisticated version of such group loyalty.

The standards of social ethics are learned primarily from an awareness of the climate of opinion. Such awareness develops during a person's upbringing, in both home and school, where manners are inculcated in the making of men and women. It is extended through social contacts of all kinds, and in modern society especially through the news media. Social ethical standards are also expressed in the legal framework of a society, both in legal codes and statutes determined by political processes and also through the precedents of case law. In all these ways the individual is subject to social pressures which condition him to conform with the ethical standards of his society.

Transcendental ethics

While standards of social ethics are determined from within any particular society, a second approach to ethics is based on absolute concepts of right and wrong which transcend all human societies. Many proponents of ethical standards have sought to establish universal concepts of goodness, rightness, justice, and so on, which could be applied equally in all human societies. In part the search for transcendental ethical standards was prompted by a realization of the weakness of social ethics in not being applicable to relations between different societies, and in part it was based on a desire to show the superiority of the ethical standards of one's own society over those of others by claiming universal applicability and truth.

More significantly, religious thinkers, prophets, priests and practitioners, many of them from backgrounds of social isolation, have proclaimed transcendental ethical standards as divine commandments. For those religions with transcendental deities, the word of God has often been expressed in concepts of correct behaviour to be observed by the entire human race. Such transcendental ethical standards are of course applicable not only within all human societies, but also in all the relations between different societies. Most world religions possess a transcendental ethos giving rise to standards of right conduct to be observed without any social limit. Similarly, there are other, non-religious philosophies, of a political, humanitarian or even materialistic nature, which give rise to transcendental ethics. By definition, this concept of ethics is fundamentally distinct from the concept of social ethics described earlier.

Tactical ethics

Many people observe ethical standards in their conduct, not because they have any great love for, or loyalty to, their own societies, their deities, or their principles, but because it suits them, whether in their private lives, their professional capacities or their business activities. Most law-abiding people observe the ethical standards embodied in legal frameworks not out of any great conviction that the law is right, but to avoid the penalties which could attend infringement of the law. Many people are happy to practise the standards of social ethics because they see this as a means of securing social advancement for themselves. Such motives may also apply in contexts where religious influences have injected measures of transcendental ethics into the predominant social ethos. In all these instances ethics

	A Keeps silent	A Confesses
B Keeps silent	A Imprisoned for one month B Imprisoned for one month Total imprisonment: two months	A Free B Imprisoned for one year Total imprisonment: one year
B Confesses	A Imprisoned for one year B Free Total imprisonment: one year	A Imprisoned for six months B Imprisoned for six months Total imprisonment: one year

Figure 4 The prisoners' dilemma

are practised out of convenience, and in pursuit of ulterior motives, most commonly the improvement and optimization of self-interest.

Ethical behaviour of this kind is certainly distinct from both the social and transcendental ethics described earlier, because it is based not on concepts of what is right in a social or absolute context, but on other considerations, as often as not what is advantageous for the individual. It is tactically beneficial to practise ethics in this way, prompted by motives which may be much less worthy than the ethical standards applied. So it seems appropriate to describe this kind of ethics as tactical ethics. In the context of the history of moral philosophy, however, such tactical ethics are close to what are generally called utilitarian ethics, a leading exponent of which, Jeremy Bentham, advocated that 'the greatest happiness of the greatest number is the foundation of morals and legislation' (Bentham 1781–5: vol. x, 142). In this context, happiness is usually equated with personal satisfaction, the fulfilment of individual self-interest, and it is the maximization of such self-interest globally which, for utilitarians, constitutes the real objective of what is to be regarded as good. Such happiness will vary according to social context and time, especially in an age like the present with such rapidly rising personal expectations and ambitions.

A well-known illustration of utilitarian ethics is the case of the 'Prisoners' Dilemma', to which Figure 4 relates. Two prisoners, A and B, have been convicted of a minor crime and are serving a month's imprisonment, but they are suspected of having jointly committed a more serious offence, for which the penalty is a year's imprisonment. Each of them is individually offered immediate release from prison if he alone admits to having committed the second crime, while there will be a sentence of only six months' imprisonment if both confess. Without confessions from either, there would be no prosecution for the second offence. Multiple sentences are to run concurrently. The dilemma facing each prisoner is then whether it is in his own interests to confess to the second crime. Figure 4 shows the consequences for both prisoners in the four sets of circumstances which could arise. For both prisoners there is the individual incentive to confess in order to be free immediately, but if they both follow this incentive they will both find their imprisonment increased from one month to six. The rational, utilitarian course of action is to minimize the total amount of imprisonment for the two men together, which is achieved by both keeping silent and not confessing. Tactical ethics requires them both to be rogues together; open honesty does not pay in the long run. However, this extends the dilemma further. If both prisoners realize that it is not in their joint interests to confess, each may assume that the other is not going to confess. There is then a real temptation for each one to break ranks and win immediate freedom at the expense of the other.

So too in many situations in life it pays to be less than honest when such honesty would reveal the dishonesty of others; but, when all are playing the game, there is the added temptation for each individual to do otherwise. Much of the current practice of business ethics is of a similar tactical nature; for instance, employees will obey codes of conduct established by their organizations when they see that such compliance will best further their own advancement within the organization, and firms will be happy to have the reputation of being 'ethical' when such a reputation attracts customers or clients.

LINKS BETWEEN THE DIFFERENT KINDS OF ETHICS

It was noted earlier that the ancient Hebrews possessed an ethical code, set out in the Pentateuch, which they regarded as expressing the will of God. So powerful was this transcendental ethos that it dominated the climate of opinion among the Jews, and thereby became their social ethos. In general they did not see this ethos as applicable to Gentiles, however, or to the relations between Jews and Gentiles. In this way the transcendental ethics of the Old Testament were changed into social ethics for most of the Jewish people, a situation to be challenged by several of the prophets such as Amos and Isaiah and, later, by Jesus Christ.

Equally there have been philosophers who have regarded religiously-based codes of transcendental ethics as really an expression of social ethics.

Montesquieu was happy to regard each society as having its own religious standards: 'When Montezuma insisted that the religion of the Spaniards was good for their country and the Mexican for his own, what he said was not absurd' (Montesquieu 1748: 24). Some social philosophers would regard religion as simply an expression of social ethos, and for them transcendental ethics is just one form of social ethics. Churches can become the vehicles of expression for the social ethos of the community around them; it used to be said, for instance, that the Church of England was the Tory Party at prayer (a claim which has been demonstrably disproved by more recent pronouncements of spokesmen of that Church). All the same, we need to be aware that what are claimed to be transcendental ethics may sometimes be social ethics in disguise.

Tactical ethics, on the other hand, are always by definition the expression of ulterior motives in the guise of either social ethics or transcendental ethics. The social climber appears to be practising social ethics but is in fact just acting selfishly. The religious hypocrite is similarly furthering his own personal interests in the clothing of transcendental ethics.

Although the practice of ethics does tend to obscure the threefold distinction which has been drawn in this chapter between social ethics, transcendental ethics and tactical ethics, it does not challenge the validity of that distinction. Furthermore, it is only with that distinction in mind that one can identify and tackle the problems of business ethics in a rigorous and logical way.

THE APPLICATION OF BUSINESS ETHICS

Every business organization adopts an ethical posture of some sort, perhaps without really being aware of it. Individuals within the organization will almost certainly have their own ethical principles, which in most cases will be distinct from, and in some cases very different from, the ethical posture of the firm. In this section we consider how principles of business ethics may be applied to guide the activities of the organization as a whole.

First, the activities of a business are subject to the law of the land, which incorporates much of the ethical standards common to society as a whole. In many respects the law is an expression of part of the framework of current social ethics, and business directors and managers who are keen to observe social ethical principles will take all possible steps to ensure that no activities of their businesses infringe the law; they would have a sense of guilt and shame if they did. But observing the law will also have some importance for business managers who have little sense of social ethics, and who are more interested in transcendental or tactical ethics. For those whose ethical principles are based on absolute concepts of what is good or right, it would be unusual if those principles were not reflected to some extent in the current state of the law, and observance of the law would to that degree equate with expression of those principles.

It might, however, be the case that on some issues the law was in opposition to some tenet of an individual's absolute ethical principles, such as on matters of freedom of access to the countryside or the right not to belong to a trade union. And for business managers who adopt a utilitarian view in ethical matters, the fact that infringement of the law will, if detected, lead to penalties for the business means that it will generally be in the firm's best interests to observe the law. It should be pointed out here, however, that instances can arise where a firm knowingly breaks the law and readily pays any penalty, having made the calculation that such penalty is more than offset by the benefits derived by the firm from breaking the law. An obvious recent example of this related to the law on Sunday trading in the UK, where some firms have deliberately traded, knowing it to be illegal, but also knowing that their financial returns from Sunday business far exceeded the level of any fines and legal costs that might be incurred. In summary, therefore, the business manager whose ethical standpoint is based on transcendental or tactical considerations will be ready to observe the law on most, though perhaps not all, occasions, while the social ethicist will conform with the law as a matter of principle.

There are, however, many outlets for the expression of social ethics other than through the law. The climate of opinion in itself is important for business, in so far as the general ethical views of society may influence demand for products marketed by a company. Strong views on the political situation in South Africa have in the past led to boycotts of South African goods and of those companies which maintained links with South Africa, and this expression of social ethics has clearly had an impact on the policies of many of those companies. Quite recently, the Church of England Synod recommended that members of that church should not buy a brand of instant coffee produced by a multinational food and beverage company, on the grounds that that company provided dried milk free to maternity hospitals and clinics in the Third World and thereby discouraged breast-feeding. While this issue is controversial, there is no doubt that the Synod action was an expression of social ethics which the company in question might need to consider carefully, if only for utilitarian reasons.

Within a profession or a sector of the economy, strength of ethical views may lead to the formulation of codes of conduct and practice to be observed by individuals or companies over and above the requirements of general law. Governments are sometimes reluctant to introduce extra legislation when they believe that the problems involved can best be tackled by regulation within the profession or industry itself. For instance the Stock Exchange has produced successive documents, known generally as the Blue, Green and Yellow Books, to regulate the activities of traders in the stock market and in the operation of mergers and take-overs of companies. While the breach of any such regulations will not in general be an illegal act, it will lead to investigation by Stock Exchange authorities and could be followed by financial penalties or expulsion from the market. In the same way most of the main professions have governing bodies which, to a greater or lesser extent, lay down rules and standards for their members to observe, and the sanctions for breaching those rules may either be financial or involve expulsion from the professional association. In these ways the expression of social ethics within the relevant part of the community brings much influence to bear on the decisions of individuals and companies, who need to take note of such ethical considerations, irrespective of their own ethical viewpoints.

The growing use of codes of conduct and practice in modern economic life has led many companies to develop ethical codes for their own staff to follow in their activities at work. The larger a company is, the more important such a code may be in communicating to all staff the ethical standards which the board of the company wishes to see observed by all employees. In some respects a code of ethics produced in this way is the expression of social ethics within the society of the company itself, and the size of that society may vary from a small handful of directors and staff, to a world-wide conglomerate. Without such a code, it may be difficult for local staff to appreciate the ethical views of a distant board running the company as a whole. Enforcement of a code of ethics within a business will almost always involve both incentives and discipline – carrots and sticks: observance of the code will stand an employee in good stead with regard to his prospects for advancement within the company, while a breach of the code will have the opposite effect and might even lead to dismissal.

Codes of ethics, however, are not necessarily easy to write or to interpret with clarity. If a company is starting from scratch in compiling a code of ethics, it is probably easiest to produce something very simple, and then to elaborate on that in the light of specific situations which arise within the running of the company. Almost always there is a need for such codes to be revised at frequent intervals. It may therefore be wisest for the code to be applied first just in one specific part of the business, where ethical problems and queries are most likely to arise, and then for it to be revised and extended several times before being applied more generally throughout the company. And whenever difficulty is experienced in interpreting a code of ethics, there is the opportunity of amending or extending the code to provide more clarity.

Finally, this chapter needs to include some reference to the problem of an individual employee of a business who finds that his or her personal ethical standards are at variance with the ethical standards applied within the company, either as general policy or by other individuals. When an individual member of staff finds that he cannot agree with the ethics of some major policy of the company which cannot be changed, then the individual will almost certainly find that he needs to seek other employment elsewhere. If the policy giving rise to the difference is not so major, or can be changed, then the individual is almost certainly justified in using whatever influence he has to seek revision of that policy; if no change comes about, the individual may then need to reconsider his own position in the light of any other opportunities open to him. Almost certainly, such a situation will involve a mixture of social, transcendental and utilitarian ethics.

Situations where an employee finds that the company, or some of his superiors within the company, are acting illegally in ways of which he personally disapproves are particularly difficult. As a general citizen, he may well feel unable to do nothing about the situation, but would only wish to report the situation to the prosecuting authorities if he had no other alternative course of action. The most likely first action for him to take would be to report the situation to his own immediate superior within the organization and discuss it with him. If that produced no change, possibly because the superior was himself involved in the illegal activity, then the employee might wish to take the matter higher, or to involve any trade union or professional association to which he belonged. Should he find that the whole company seemed involved in the illicit activity, then he might have no alternative but to report the position to the police and seek alternative employment for himself. 'Whistle-blowing' actions like this are increasingly evident, especially in the United States, and recent celebrated cases have shown the need for them.

In maintaining ethical standards within a business company, the roles of shareholders and non-executive directors are important, for they do not generally derive their main income from the operations of the company, and can bring pressure to bear from more objective viewpoints. And of course shareholders as the owners of the company and board members as the policy-makers are in the long run in good positions to wield influence.

Chapter 6

Business and financial and fiscal institutions

The operations of any business organization are constrained by the financial requirements of the community in which it operates, and by the financial framework ordained by the traditions and politics of that community. We saw in Chapter 2 how the British economy can properly be described as a mixed economy, and in this chapter we shall examine how any business in the UK relates to the financial institutions which make up much of the framework of the national economy. Although the chapter confines its attention to the UK alone, as with previous chapters it is true to say that there are other countries, particularly within the Commonwealth, with similar financial structures and institutions.

There are two kinds of institution to be considered. First, there are the revenue-raising agencies of the national exchequer, namely the Inland Revenue and Customs and Excise, and any successful business has to be fully aware of the need to meet its obligations towards them. Second, however, there are financial institutions with an ostensibly more positive role in assisting businesses with financial help, the joint-stock banks and merchant banks, the Stock Exchange and the increasingly important institutional investors.

THE AGENCIES FOR COLLECTION OF PUBLIC REVENUE

In Chapter 3 reference was made to the constraints on business of Acts of Parliament which have become law during the lifetimes of successive governments. Many of these Acts are of a fiscal nature, relating to the need to raise revenue to finance public expenditure, both at national and at local level, and this legislation imposes obligations on businesses no less than on individual citizens. Indeed, the fact that companies have had legal entity since 1844 has made it possible for them to be subject, as corporate bodies, to specific forms of taxation, and they are corporately liable if they fail to meet those financial obligations. Much political pressure is brought to bear on government and Parliament by business organizations, for example the Confederation of British Industry or the Forum for Small

Business, when there are proposals to introduce new taxes or to increase existing ones. In the democratic structure of the UK, businesses have the same rights as individuals to make their views known on such issues of public policy, except of course that businesses have no voting rights. Much of the taxation legislation to which businesses are subject is contained in the annual Finance Acts which implement the Chancellor's Budget proposals, but there are other relevant Acts, particularly when a new form of tax is introduced or when existing legislation is consolidated.

In the UK, businesses are subject to both national and local taxation. National taxes may be in the form of either direct taxation, assessed and collected by the Inland Revenue from businesses directly as a result of their profits, or they may be in the form of indirect taxation, arising from particular trading activities, irrespective of whether or not they produce a profit for the business. While some small one-man businesses may be required to pay only income tax and national insurance contributions in respect of their business profits, direct taxation on businesses is now largely in the form of corporation tax, while indirect taxation may be in the form of value added tax (VAT), customs duty, excise duty of one form or another, or car tax. Figure 5 shows the amounts of these taxes collected in the 1990/91 financial year. Corporation tax is levied directly on businesses as legal entities in their own right, while the other taxes mentioned are levied on particular trading activities of businesses. The agency responsible for collecting corporation tax is the Inland Revenue, through its district inspectors of taxes and collectors of taxes, while the agency responsible for collecting the indirect taxes is HM Customs and Excise, which includes the local VAT offices. Local taxation, on the other hand, is now in the form of the Uniform Business Tax, the one part of the general rating system which has, to date, survived all the recent changes in the financing of local government, and which involves assessments of business premises by rating and valuation officers and collection by the finance departments of local district councils. We shall now describe the operations of all these taxation agencies in detail, one by one.

Every business organization is legally required to fulfil specific statutory obligations towards the Inland Revenue. The first such duty is to notify the office of the local district inspector of taxes of the existence of the business and of its potential taxability. Second, the business is legally required to complete an annual return of income so that its liability for tax can be assessed; this duty will usually be discharged by completion of the forms sent to the business by the Revenue. Third, if the business has paid employees, it is legally required to operate the Pay-As-You-Earn (PAYE) scheme for deducting income tax and national insurance contributions at source from salary and wage payments and then sending that tax directly to the Revenue. Similarly, income tax is to be deducted at source by companies from dividend payments made to shareholders,

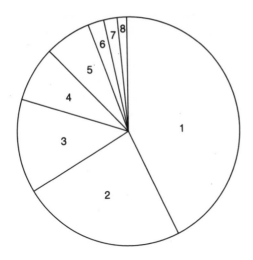

£ millions

1	Value added tax	31,005.7	42.8%
2	Corporations tax	17,136.0	23.7%
3	Hydrocarbon oil tax	9,628.1	13.3%
4	Tobacco duty	5,636.0	7.8%
5	Alcohol duties	4,855.9	6.7%
6	Customs duty	1,684.1	2.3%
7	Car tax	1,463.7	2.0%
8	Betting and gaming duty	1,006.4	1.4%

Figure 5 Taxes collected from businesses in the UK, 1990–1

Note: The source of the above information for corporation tax is the Report of the Board of Inland Revenue for the year ending 31 March 1991 (Cmd 1767), and the figure for that tax is the amount collected in the year ending 31 October 1990. The source for all the other taxes and duties is the Report of HM Customs and Excise for 1990/1 (Cm. 1636), which gives the figures for net receipts in the year ending 31 March 1991.

and from interest payments in respect of loans made to the company, all such deductions being at the standard rate of tax. Businesses in the construction industry are also required by statute to operate the Construction Industry Deduction Scheme by making deductions from payments to labour-only sub-contractors. Finally, any business is required by the Taxes Management Act 1970 to meet any request from the Inland Revenue for information about other companies or individuals about their taxable income, and about payments made to others about services or as interest.

All these obligations towards the Inland Revenue have the full force of law, and penalties may be imposed on businesses failing to meet them. Similarly, when a company is late in paying tax to the Inland Revenue, interest may be added at specified rates by the Revenue to the amounts overdue. It is therefore very much in a company's interests to handle all its tax affairs in proper order and to be fully open in all dealings with the Inland Revenue, whose officers are required to be considerate and fair, as well as thorough and correct in all their work. The Taxpayers' Charter, introduced in 1986, applies to businesses as well as individual taxpayers, and spells out the rights of all taxpayers to fair treatment, confidentiality, and of appeal to independent Commissioners or, if necessary, to the courts. The complexity of tax matters, however, means that it is almost certainly necessary for a business to have professional help in all dealings with the Revenue, either through seeking the services of professional accountants or by directly employing such financial expertise. The question as to when it is better to employ in-house accountants depends on the circumstances of individual companies, and similar factors apply to this as were considered in Chapter 4 with regard to the employment of in-house lawyers.

The services of professional accountants can be particularly useful to a company in helping to plan its operations so as to minimize its overall legitimate tax liability, both by ensuring that all possible reliefs against tax are claimed, and by the timing of those expenses which can be set against profit to best effect. Certain business operations are tax-efficient while others are not, and what may seem to be the most profitable policy for a company to follow may not be so after the tax implications have been taken into account. While the Inland Revenue has neither a legal nor a moral obligation to advise any business on these matters, they can have no objection – and are usually very appreciative of the situation – when a company so organizes its affairs to minimize its tax liability.

Similar considerations apply in respect of the Customs and Excise, whose operations are similarly covered by the Taxpayers' Charter. Most business organizations are liable to pay VAT in respect of their activities, and we turn now to consider how a business can most efficiently discharge its obligations in respect of this form of indirect taxation.

VAT is incurred on a very wide range of business transactions, including sales of many commodities and services, hiring of goods, admission to premises, and facilities provided by clubs. Some transactions are statutorily exempt from VAT, such as insurance premiums, medical services or some supplies provided by undertakers. Those transactions which are not exempt are known as taxable supplies, all of which are subject to VAT at a specified rate of tax, including the zero rate and the standard rate, which was increased by the Finance Act 1991 to 17½ per cent. Zero-rated supplies at present include most provision of food (but not catering or restaurant services), books and newspapers, new housing, young children's clothing and all exports. In general, businesses are required to add the standard rate of VAT to charges made in respect of all non-exempt, non zero-rated business supplies which they provide.

The first question facing any business in respect of VAT is whether there is a requirement to register for the tax. Such registration may be in the name of the sole proprietor of a business, or the name of a partnership, a limited company, a club or association or a charity. The law requires that all businesses be registered for VAT whose total annual taxable turnover, i.e. income from standard and zero-rated supplies, exceeds a specified amount, which as of 11 March 1992 was £36,600, and which is subject to frequent, though not necessarily annual, alteration. While registration imposes an obligation on a business to charge VAT on its taxable supplies, it also enables the business to reclaim the VAT it has itself paid on chargeable supplies which it has received and used in the making of its own taxable supplies; the amount of VAT which the business actually pays to the VAT office is the excess of the tax on its output over the tax paid on its input. For instance, a company manufacturing furniture will be charged VAT on the wood it uses to make furniture, but it may reclaim this when paying the VAT it has charged when selling the finished furniture. The circumstances of a business may sometimes be such that its VAT on output is less than its VAT on input, and then registration will enable the business to reclaim the difference from Customs and Excise; for instance, a building firm pays VAT on its supplies of materials, bricks, cement, etc., but it does not need to charge VAT on new residential buildings it constructs, and, in such a case, it may be due a net refund of VAT. The benefit of being able to reclaim VAT in such circumstances is also available to businesses, including charities, which have an annual taxable turnover below the registration threshold, but which are allowed to register voluntarily because the VAT they pay on input exceeds any amount they may charge on output. Consequently it may be in the interests of a business to register for VAT even if its taxable turnover is less than £36,600.

In order to register for VAT, contact should be made with the local VAT office, as listed in the local telephone directory under Customs and Excise. That office will then set in motion the procedure for allocating a VAT registration number to the business, and for supplying the business with a VAT return form every three months, to be completed with details of all VAT transactions during the previous quarter and returned to the VAT Central Unit at Southend with any VAT that may be payable. To complete returns accurately it is necessary to keep a record of all VAT transactions from the date the business first became required to register for VAT. Keeping such records and accounts can be complicated and time-consuming, but is necessary in order to satisfy VAT inspectors that the quarterly returns are correct. Customs and Excise provide guidance about their requirements in this respect, and special schemes are available to simplify the arrangements for certain retail trades. In any case, because accounts are required from the very date on which a firm becomes eligible for VAT registration and the firm will need to pay VAT in respect of all its transactions from that date, it is in the firm's interests to ensure that it charges VAT on all its taxable supplies from the same date.

Once a business is registered for VAT, it will receive a constant supply of literature and forms from the VAT Central Unit, which should leave managers and staff of the business in no doubt as to what is required of them in respect of VAT. While businesses are expected to be conversant with legal requirements affecting them, they should never hesitate to seek advice from the VAT office named in their VAT certificate. Getting things wrong can cost money, in the form of penalties.

From time to time, registered businesses will be visited by VAT inspectors whose purpose is to check that the business is handling its VAT affairs correctly and returning all due tax. On such visits VAT inspectors will need access to full records and accounts. In the event of a dispute arising over the VAT liability of a business, the firm may exercise its right of appeal against any decision of the local VAT inspector, such appeal being directed in the first instance to the local VAT office, with a reasoned request for reconsideration of the case; if the firm remains dissatisfied, its appeal can then be lodged with a VAT appeal tribunal. As noted earlier, the Taxpayers' Charter applies to Customs and Excise; VAT officers are required to be courteous and fair in all their dealings, as well as thorough and accurate. It needs to be remembered that the Taxpayers' Charter also expects taxpayers to be accurate and honest!

The other taxes collected by Customs and Excise relate either to imported goods or to particular supplies such as cars, hydrocarbon oils, alcohol, tobacco, or betting and gaming, and any business manager involved with making such supplies will need to ensure that his firm is fulfilling its tax obligations in those respects. Again it pays to be open and frank in maintaining a good relationship with the relevant local office of Customs and Excise.

The contribution which business organizations now make to local government finance in the UK is through payment of the Uniform Business Tax (UBT), which continues as one surviving element of the general rating system which generally disappeared in 1990. (Water charges for most residential properties are also still based on the old rating assessments of those properties.) For UBT, every set of business premises is assessed by the district valuer and valuation officer, a civil servant employed by national government, in accordance with what rent the premises might command on the open property market, any scarcity factor having been deducted. Throughout England and Wales there has recently been a full revaluation of all business premises in this way. Firms which dispute the accuracy of the assessment of their premises have the right of appeal to rating appeal tribunals. Once the assessment is fixed for particular premises, the amount of UBT to be paid in any year for those premises is determined by the settling by national government of the uniform rate to be paid for every pound of the assessment. The amount so calculated is then collected by the district council in whose area the premises are situated, and is immediately transferred to a single national pool, for redistribution to local authorities, both county and district councils, in accordance with their needs and the levels of local demands for their services. It is therefore no longer a direct benefit to a local authority to have rateable business premises within its area, and the mechanisms of UBT are used by national government to redistribute local government revenue from one part of the country to another. Equally, because the business rate is uniform throughout the country, the levels of local government rates no longer act as incentives or discentives to firms to set up premises in one part of the country rather than another. All the same, any business needs to make sure that it is meeting its obligations fully and promptly in respect of UBT.

INSTITUTIONS WHICH PROVIDE FINANCE

Small businesses in need of capital to finance new development will in most cases turn first to the local branch of their joint-stock bank, consulting the branch manager or a specialist in arranging such financial advances. Although there has recently been much controversy about the attitudes of joint-stock banks towards small businesses, the leading banks like Midland or National Westminster do have special sections and schemes for helping small businesses, and their larger branches have specialist staff trained to deal with such matters. Because many of the banks have recently lost money by lending to unsuccessful businesses (and countries!) and have had to write-off large amounts of such losses, they exercise particular care in considering applications for loans. For such consideration they require detailed information from the business about why the loan is requested, how it will be used and how it will be repaid. This usually means that the bank needs a full statement of the business plans of the firm. It is also in the firm's interests not to be overstretched in carrying loans, in terms of either the total size of loans or the levels of interest to be paid. Bank loans to most businesses are on the basis of interest payments at several percentage points above the Bank of England base rate; only well-established and large 'blue-chip' companies can attract bank loans at interest rates anywhere close to base rate. Loans become crippling liabilities when the repayments plus interest on them each year takes up most of the income which the loans have enabled the business to generate, or when they cannot be repaid during the lifetime of the plant acquired with them. It is always risky to raise loans to purchase depreciating assets, and most business equipment declines in value, while land or buildings tend to appreciate. Loans to acquire property or 'real estate' are always safer than loans to acquire equipment, so long as the property market is stable.

Most of the funding of business companies in the United Kingdom is generated internally from profits. For example, in 1988, bank borrowings accounted for only 24.14 per cent of the total funding of the 1,560 largest public companies, while the issue of shares brought in another 14.55 per cent (Annual Abstract of Statistics, 1991, section 17.26). All the same, there are times when the provision of share capital is essential to a company's development, and guidance and advice from merchant banks are required.

When a private company wishes to expand far beyond the limits of the means of its current shareholders, it needs to apply to become a Public Limited Company (PLC), with its shares to be traded on the Stock Exchange and usually quoted daily in the press, or to be included in either the Unlisted Securities Market (USM), introduced in 1980, or the Section 353 Market consisting of small public companies whose share prices are not quoted on a daily basis. Going public in any of these ways is a formidable operation for any private company, with the value of the company and of all shareholdings to be determined in future by the public market. Only occasionally does a company which has gone public later return to private status; when this does happen, as in the case of the Really Useful Group, the original private owners usually wish to regain control over the running of the company and are in a position to buy back all the shares sold on the public market at the price asked by their new holders. Going public means that the control of the company may pass from the original private owners, especially if there is a take-over of the company's shares on the market.

Consequently, any firm considering going public needs expert advice about the risks involved and the steps to be taken. In most cases this advice is obtained from professional merchant bankers. In order to offer advice, the bankers will need to undertake their own survey of the strength of the company and make their own assessment of its potential value; in this process the directors may well feel that they are being taken over by the bankers! But in every step of the flotation the advice of the bankers could be crucial, especially if the market at the time is volatile. The role of merchant banks in this way has become much more visible to the public in recent years because of the government's privatization programme, in which firms of merchant banks have steered the entire operation. Sometimes they have misjudged the market, notably when the remaining tranche of the government's shareholding in BP was put on the market in October 1987, when the general crash on the Stock Market came between the setting of the share price and the actual date of the sale. The result was that the sale was a flop; the few investors who did buy shares all lost heavily, and the Bank of England intervened to buy shares to stem the fall in the share price.

Supervising flotations is one part of the corporate finance activity of merchant banks, where they are not employing their funds and capital, but are providing a service for which they earn fees. Such activity also includes the provision of advice and professional service in proposals for company mergers and take-overs. In particular, merchant banks providing advice in such circumstances should ensure that there is compliance with all the rules and regulations governing the situation in question. Rules for full flotation of companies on the Stock Market are contained in the loose-leafed 'Yellow Book', *Admission of Securities to Listing*, while the corresponding document for the USM is popularly known as the 'Green Book'. Extending the colour scheme further, there is a 'Blue Book' called *City Code on Take-overs and Mergers*, which lists the rules governing acquisitions and details the need to avoid insider dealing and to construct 'Chinese Walls' to prevent irregular trading. Recent well-publicized cases in this area have increased public awareness of the temptations to indulge in unethical or even illegal conduct in share transactions, probably contravening the Prevention of Fraud (Securities) Act. The Stock Exchange is clearly anxious that its own codes of regulations are observed, to avoid any necessity for more general legislation to be enacted and enforced by the courts.

Providing advice and service in corporate finance has become the main role of the merchant banks. As their name implies, they started off as traditional bankers, receiving deposits from wealthy clients and lending that money at profitable rates of interest. But as bankers, merchant banks are all much smaller than the high street clearing banks, whose lending and borrowing business is mainly counter-driven, with loans and deposits recoverable on demand. By contrast, merchant banks usually raise money on a committed, fixed-term basis, and they lend that money at a specified margin above the London Inter-Bank Operating Rate (LIBOR). While the clearing banks might be regarded as retailers serving the general public, the merchant banks are more like wholesalers, accepting only very large deposits, often from clearing banks or other financial institutions. Some, but not all, merchant banks are themselves PLCs with listed shares, and the income produced by their operations may be added to their capital bases or distributed to shareholders as in any other company. In providing banking services, as in most of their activities, most merchant banks are also active at an international level, providing advice on the transfer of funds from one country to another and on all aspects of currency dealing.

The third main area of merchant banking activity is in asset or fund management, whereby the capital of wealthy clients is administered by the merchant bank; to qualify for such service the client generally needs minimum capital of £500,000, which excludes all but a few private individuals, but includes many institutional investors such as unit trusts and investment trusts. The merchant bank will advise the customer on how most profitably to invest the capital, whether in stocks and shares or otherwise.

The importance of institutional investors

Although it was estimated that, at the end of 1991, there were 12.7 million individual investors in the UK, some 70 per cent of capital on the Stock Exchange is owned by institutions, notably the pension funds of large employers and insurance companies, or investment trusts and unit trusts. The largest pension fund in the country is the British Coal pension fund, with assets of £12.6 billions, while the Universities Superannuation Scheme is the sixth largest with assets of £4.9 billion (*Sunday Times*, 8 December, 1991). Through such institutions millions of private individuals have a stake in the stock market, and the funds of the institutions have come to dominate the market, accounting for the major shareholding of most public companies, and equally importantly, most early trading in securities. The movement of institutional funds on the Stock Market has far more influence on the level of share prices than the purchases and sales of individual investors, and any public company needs to retain the goodwill of its large institutional shareholders. The voices of institutions can be dominant in the business of annual meetings of companies and in the appointment of board members. It is noticeable how, for many of the companies privatized in the 1980s, the initial large number of individual shareholders declined fairly quickly as they sold their shares at a premium, mainly to institutional investors.

Of course, the funds of institutional investors belong ultimately to millions of private individuals, who see this method of investing their savings as an opportunity to spread their investment risk and enjoy the benefit of the financial strength of the institutions in the market. While, from the viewpoint of a company, the institutions may appear to have become omnipotent in the market, from the viewpoint of an individual these giants provide some degree of welcome protection against the vagaries of the market and the rashness of some company decisions. All the same, widespread public concern about the ethics of large-scale financial operations by companies led to the setting up in 1991 of the Cadbury Committee on Corporate Governance, to investigate general allegations of boardroom greed, the morality of take-over practices and the role of non-executive directors.

Chapter 7

Business and technology

THE IMPORTANCE OF TECHNOLOGY

No one should underestimate the significance of technology in influencing the whole lifestyle of a community. Here the term 'technology' is taken to have the broad meaning of 'the practical application of methods of using physical resources'. The state of technology in any community therefore depends on the availability of those physical resources and, even more, on the knowledge and skill of those able to use those resources. Technology changes as new physical resources are discovered, as knowledge develops with new discoveries and inventions, and as experience applies techniques in one field of human activity which have been developed in others. Changes in technology produce completely new commodities to be marketed and completely new methods for their manufacture and distribution and for the whole operation of business companies.

But the impact of technological change extends far more widely than just in producing new items to be manufactured or new methods for conducting business. It influences the whole nature of society, causing social and political change, local, national and international. From the invention of the wheel to the latest development of laser surgery, technology has probably caused more change in human affairs than all the efforts of politicians and political thinkers together. The agricultural revolution of the eighteenth century, with the introduction of new methods of farming and new machinery, changed the pattern of land tenure, enclosing the commons and fields of strip cultivation, and started the depopulation of the countryside, with fewer and fewer people drawing their livelihoods from agriculture. The industrial revolution, with the invention of new textile machinery and of the steam engine, provided more and more employment in urban and industrialized areas, creating pressure for political reform and the widening of the franchise. The subsequent transport revolution facilitated mobility of labour and opened up vast new markets across the world, creating a new community of nations.

In recent years the continuing revolution in telecommunications has brought the whole world closer together, with instant relay of news across the earth, the dissemination of information to peoples previously in ignorance of what was happening elsewhere, and the raising of their material and political expectations as they have come to see, on television, the standards of living enjoyed by others. More than any other factor, television has been responsible for the changes in eastern Europe and the Soviet Union during the late 1980s and early 1990s. This was so particularly in Germany, where the pressure for reunification was due not so much to the efforts of politicians as to the impact of German-language television displaying to the East the benefits of the free economy in the West.

Technological change can be so sweeping and powerful that its impact is unwelcome to many, especially those with deep vested interests in the established order, who see their livelihoods threatened by the introduction of new methods and products. In 1782 a Leicestershire hosiery worker, Ned Ludd, used violent methods to destroy a stocking-frame which his employer had introduced into his place of work and which Ludd regarded as a substitute for himself. The Luddite riots in the years after 1810, when gangs of employees in the industrial Midlands and North of England smashed up new machinery which they saw as threatening their employment prospects were an expression of the resistance to technological innovation which is present in every age. Business managers who need no persuasion about the benefits of new technology to their operations and their profitability may still find great difficulty in persuading their workforce likewise.

In considering the impact of technological change on their businesses, managers therefore need to be aware of the potential new products which new technology can supply, of the new methods of production and business operation which have become technically and financially feasible, and of the implications which such changes may have in terms of personnel management and industrial relations in their companies. These three areas will now be considered more fully in turn.

Technology and new products

The success of any business depends on how far it can continue to provide a supply which meets market demand, and on how far it is able to maintain and expand its share of the market for that supply. Technological change may create demand for new products and reduce demand for old products. The adaptation of products by new technology may give a business a crucial competitive edge over rival producers. Consequently it is essential for business managers to be aware of how technological change is affecting demand for their products and is creating opportunities for new products to be supplied for which there is a ready market. Much of this awareness will come through the collection of market information, either in the form of surveys of customer opinion about existing products and how they might be adapted, or of knowledge of what competitors are providing and planning.

When market information indicates a potential demand for an adapted product or a new product, the successful business needs to direct its energy to finding ways of producing a supply to meet that demand. In a small firm this search may depend on using the ingenuity of individual employees; in larger firms it will be the responsibility of research and development departments. The nature of such departments will vary according to the products of the company, but almost certainly they will include scientific or engineering expertise. With the rapid advances in technological innovation, it is unlikely that any business can continue to be successful for long without some facilities for research and development of products. This does not mean that successful new products are bound to be more technically complicated than those they replace; sometimes new products can be deceptively simple, like dental cement or new kinds of adhesive paper, but usually their simplicity is the result of many years of professional technological research.

It is sometimes debated whether the initiative in launching new products should rest with the technical researchers and inventors or with market surveyors. The answer of course is that both must be involved, for neither group can be successful without the other. If market research shows that there is a definite demand for a new kind of product at present not on the market, an incentive exists for technical personnel to try to develop such a product; conversely, if a new or adapted product is invented by technical staff, market research needs to be undertaken to ascertain what likely demand there is for it. It is only when business managers know that they have a new product and a market for it that they can realistically decide to invest in its supply.

The importance of research and development has been stressed by many modern industrialists, who see these activities as the only way of keeping abreast or ahead of competitors over the years to come. However, the provision of adequate research and development facilities can be expensive, especially in the employment of specialist personnel, and there is usually no immediate financial return for this investment. When a firm is small, it may not be practical to have a research and development department internal to the business. In those circumstances, the business will need to use external consultants in developing new products, either in consultancy firms or in departments of universities and other scientific institutions. Often such consultancy will arise when market information has indicated that there is a clear demand for a specified new type of product. Equally there have been examples of new inventions within scientific and engineering laboratories which have never been commercially exploited, and links between industry and such scientific bodies may lead to the proper development of their market potential.

The whole field of technology transfer in the UK has a chequered history, and there have been examples where inventions by British scientists and engineers have not been exploited with sufficient speed in this country to outstrip foreign competitors. The history of the National Research Development Corporation and its successor, the British Technology Group, in this field has shown delays in the evaluation of new inventions, on average two years long, and bureaucracy has tended to stifle enterprise. In 1983, however, the monopoly of the British Technology Group in the commercial transfer of new technology was ended, and since then other independent companies have entered the field. All the same, the successful transfer of technology to full commercial exploitation depends to a large extent on the enterprise of business managers in taking on new ventures which may involve financial risk. There is no doubt that success in this field is assisted by the maintenance of a close and constructive relationship between a business company and appropriate scientific or engineering departments in the academic sector.

Technology and new methods

In the same way, most businesses need to be aware of the potential created by new technology for changes in the methods used within the business, whether in the production of commodities or in the internal service functions of the business itself. Sometimes the introduction of new products will itself dictate that new machinery needs to be installed and operated for their manufacture. On other occasions, new machinery will be invented to produce the same goods in a more efficient or less expensive way than the old machinery. This applies particularly to the introduction of robotic methods to lines of mass production, as in the manufacture of motor cars. At other times the adaptation of a product will necessitate a corresponding adaptation of the plant used in its production. Perhaps such a change may arise as a suggestion from some enterprising member of the firm's own workforce, or it may be suggested by external consultants. New production machinery may appear on the market which the firm can acquire, or it may be invented in a scientific or engineering department. In all these ways, business managers need to maintain a close awareness of all the potential technical changes for their production processes. Such awareness may involve the use of suggestion boxes in the workplace, the constant scanning of trade magazines, as well as patient listening to the sales talk of machinery suppliers and a continuing relationship with sources of new technology relevant to their processes.

While the development of new technology in some specialized fields of manufacture will be very important for the businesses within such fields, of far wider application are technological changes in business methods generally, in the areas of communication, information management and financial transfer. Almost every business has in recent years gone through the transition from typewriters, carbon paper and extensive paper records to word processors, photocopiers, fax machines, computer storage of data and computer production of invoices and accounts. While such changes may involve substantial capital outlay, in general they all lead to greater business efficiency, the facilitation of business decisions and ease of storage of records. The efficient processing of information is now generally accepted as a key input to business growth. Whereas in the past the internal services of a business were usually labour-intensive, involving the employment of large numbers of secretaries, typists and clerks, the coming together of computers and telecommunications has created a more capital-intensive base for the fast and world-wide transfer of information.

This applies in particular to businesses in the financial world: building societies, banks of all kinds, dealers in stocks and shares, insurance dealers, and so on. The use of credit cards has facilitated electronic transfer of funds, enabling traders to receive payment for their goods and services immediately. Even where cheques are still in use for financial transfer, they can be cleared almost as soon as they have been banked. Large firms are now able to operate accounting systems on a corporation-wide basis, continuously updated to the moment, and many systems of expert information are electronically available to assist decision making by businesses. Of course this abundance of electronic aids brings its own problems, especially in the field of security of confidential information, the protection of computer systems against breakdowns and viruses, and in the sheer overloading of information, with managers unable to reach decisions quickly because they cannot extract the vital information from the mass available.

The financial markets have experienced a trading revolution due to the introduction of this new technology. Dealers in stocks and shares are now able to make transactions from their desks with their arrays of computer screens, rather than amid the clamour of the crowded stock exchange floor, and the mere presence of all the technology has at once made markets more volatile. As soon as a share price shows a small dip, this information is immediately flashed across the screens of the market, triggering off other decisions by investors either to buy or to sell. The crash on the world's stock markets in October 1987 was due in no small measure to the application of all the new technology, whereby decisions to sell shares when their price fell to a certain level had been stored on computers and were automatically activated as the market fell headlong. Equally, the same processes may assist sudden rises in the market.

Another field where electronic innovation has led to a revolution in business methods is in large retailing outlets such as supermarkets. The delays involved in customers queuing to pay for their purchases at the check-out tills of supermarkets have been reduced because assistants no longer have to ring up the prices of individual purchases; goods are specially marked so that they can be 'read' by machine and their prices added to the customer's total. This process, known as electronic point of sale, or EPOS, also enables a computer record to be kept of sales, advising managers when stocks of a commodity are running out on the shelves and helping them to decide the size of batches to be ordered to meet demand in the short-term future. This not only enables decisions to be reached in making orders, but less staff need be involved in the process of checking how much of a commodity is still in stock. This is one example of the personnel implications of the use of new technology; we now turn to consider that aspect of technological innovation in more detail.

Technology and personnel relations

It was noted earlier that Luddite rioters some 200 years ago deliberately destroyed new machinery because they regarded it as a threat to their own livelihoods. Much technological innovation poses a similar threat to the vested interests of established labour and its introduction is likely to be resisted, hopefully not with violence, but by strong industrial relations pressure and action. Any business manager considering the introduction of new technology needs first to work out how to do this with least turbulence in industrial relations.

Much of the development of new products and new machinery will involve no need to reduce manpower in a business overall, but will require existing employees to adapt to new methods of work and sometimes to be completely redeployed to new tasks. In the majority of cases this can be achieved smoothly, provided there is a sympathetic approach by management to the difficulties arising for the staff who are involved, and provided there is proper provision for retraining, with adequate instruction so that staff may know what is required of them. For instance, many secretaries have successfully made the transition from typewriters to word processors after attending seminars and short courses on the use of their new machines. No good manager will require staff to switch to new machinery without suitable training in this way, and often it is advisable to provide incentives in the form of enhanced rates of pay or productivity bonuses. Where the workforce is organized in trade unions or with a system of employee representatives, these arrangements will require very careful and patient negotiation if the introduction of new technology is to be implemented successfully.

More difficult is the situation where technological innovation causes redundancy among staff because their skills will no longer be required and there will be no opportunities for them to be redeployed within the firm. This is bound to happen whenever new technology changes a labour-intensive operation into a capital-intensive one. To some extent this happened in much of the British newspaper industry during the 1980s. Large numbers of compositors and others employed in the manual setting of type were replaced by computerized systems enabling journalists to compose their copy on word-processor screens for automatic transfer to the sub-editors, who were similarly using computers electronically to make up the actual newspaper pages. This situation gave rise to a major industrial relations confrontation, with the graphical trades unions totally opposed to reductions in the labour force (which would, of course, lead to reductions in their own membership). So entrenched were the opposing positions in this dispute that some leading newspaper proprietors decided to move their operations away from their traditional premises in Fleet Street with the associated chapels of organized labour. Completely fresh operations were set up in the East End of London and elsewhere where the industrial relations framework could be reconstructed from scratch. This led to the famous scenes of violent picketing at Wapping which ended only after police action and after it had become clear that the pickets could achieve nothing. These events were perhaps the clearest manifestations of Luddism in modern times.

So what can managers do to minimize such difficulties when technological innovation will necessitate a reduction in the workforce? There can be no substitute for thorough consultation with staff representatives and for making every attempt to negotiate agreements, offering productivity bonuses and generous redundancy terms, and endeavouring to phase in essential redundancies over a period of perhaps several years, so that individuals can have time to adapt and find alternative employment. On the other side, staff representatives need to accept the advantages of new technology and to seek to negotiate conditions for its introduction which will cushion their members against the resulting disruptive effects. In this situation of collective bargaining, there needs to be flexibility on all sides to avoid damaging the interests of all. History shows that the world does not stand still, and no one can expect to stop the introduction of new technology, with all its advantages for the community at large. Nevertheless, in industrial relations it takes 'two to tango', and an obstructive attitude on either side can be met by the other side only by confrontation or capitulation, neither of which is good for all concerned. In such circumstances the relocation of premises by newspaper proprietors seemed like a reasonable alternative.

The first part of this chapter demonstrated the importance of technological change in bringing about economic, social and political change in the lives of communities, of nations and of the whole world. It is no wonder therefore that new technology can have drastic and painful effects for thousands of individuals whose work is affected by it. Just as the agricultural and industrial revolutions reshaped the destinies of nations in their own day, so the changes brought about by the microchip and by electronic communications are now causing revolutions in the whole lifestyles of business organizations, of managers, employees and customers alike. It is not an overstatement to say that the human race has never before seen so much change taking place at once and with such rapidity. The management of such change calls for immense skill in running business organizations.

Chapter 8

Business and demography

THE IMPORTANCE OF PEOPLE FOR BUSINESS

In the same way as there is a constantly expanding availability of new technology to be used in commercial development, so also the human impact on any business is continually changing. No business will survive, let alone prosper, unless there is a clear recognition that its strength depends upon people, whether as consumers, employees, shareholders, suppliers or stakeholders of any other kind. As the population changes, so there will be changes in the impact which that population has on businesses, and any successful business needs to take account of those changes and to adapt its activities accordingly. If people are living longer, or retiring earlier, or marrying later, or having smaller families, the composition of society as a whole changes, with consequent changes in the patterns of consumer demand, in the structure of the labour market, in the output of the educational process, and in lifestyles generally. Successful businesses must be able to go with the grain of such changes, adapting products to new markets, adapting recruitment and personnel policies, and reflecting the changing social ethos within which they operate. In short, any business is part and parcel of the whole society to which it belongs, and demographic changes in that society are bound to influence the way the business is conducted.

It was noted in Chapter 2 that the interrelationship between business and population was seen, if not entirely accurately, as long ago as the end of the eighteenth century by Thomas Malthus. His gloomy 'iron law of population' predicted that the growth of population would always tend to outstrip economic growth, with the result that the general standard of living would never rise. In the developed world, Malthus has been proved wrong because economic development has generally proceeded apace, while in the second half of the twentieth century voluntary birth control has contributed to stability in the total size of the population. Elsewhere in the world, however, Malthus's theory can be widely seen in reality, especially in famine-stricken regions like Bangladesh and sub-Saharan

Africa. More significant for our present discussion is the way in which Malthus perceived that there is a potential interaction between demographic and economic changes. Far from being an abstract science, economics is essentially one of the humanities relating primarily to people. Similarly, any successful businessman or woman needs to recognize that commercial activity is basically about people, and when the structure of population changes there will almost certainly be major implications for business.

The rest of this chapter will concentrate on the demographic changes that have been taking place in the UK during the last twenty years, and which continue to do so, in common with similar trends in other developed western countries. In brief, those trends involve a steadily increasing life expectancy due to the effects of medicine, diet, the absence of major wars and other catastrophes, a tendency to retire earlier due to redundancy and employment policies and the effect of technological changes, a decline in the birth rate due to widespread birth control and changes in marital and family patterns, and the growing equality of men and women in economic and social activity. These factors all bear fundamentally on the nature of markets for goods and services, and especially on the labour markets. We turn now to consider each of them in more detail.

The increase in life expectancy

In the census of 1851 it was discovered that 4.6 per cent of the population of Great Britain was made up of people aged sixty-five and over; by 1981 that proportion had increased to 15.1 per cent. (This information and much of what follows in this section of the chapter is drawn from Chapter 5 in Joshi 1989.) It is projected that this proportion will increase to between 16.8 and 20 per cent by the year 2025. In absolute terms, there were 2.4 million 'elderly' people, that is men over sixty-five and women over sixty, in the United Kingdom in 1901, and by 1977 the figure had increased to 9.6 millions, with 2.9 millions of those over the age of seventy-five. If present trends continue, it is projected that the average life expectancy of a child born in the UK in the year 2000 will be over eighty years; as that figure is an average, many of those children will live to be centenarians.

People are living longer because of the success of the medical professions in overcoming the diseases and ailments which brought about earlier death in the past. Furthermore, better food and a greater variety of food have improved people's general health, so that they are less prone to illnesses and physical deterioration. Similarly, environmental improvements have reduced vulnerability to disease – particularly improvements in conditions of employment and in control of atmospheric pollution. Social pressures are constantly at work to reduce the incidence of fatal and other accidents of all kinds, and the massive loss of human life in war and armed conflict is now hopefully a matter of history alone. The work of surgeons, doctors, nurses, environmentalists, social pioneers and politicians has all contributed to the successful extension of the average span of life. Almost everybody will regard this as a cause of great rejoicing and congratulation.

The fact that more and more people are living longer has far-reaching social implications. While death may have been postponed for most people, old age may still be accompanied by physical weakness and disability and by debilitating illnesses which are not fatal. Caring for the elderly is one of the growth sectors in the modern economy, with substantial increases in the number of residential homes for the elderly and units of sheltered accommodation. Whereas in previous generations the normal social pattern was for elderly relatives to be cared for in the same homes as their families, geographical mobility now prevents that from happening so much, and wider social provision is required. Furthermore the development of techno-logical aids for the elderly, particularly in the field of intercommunicating systems, has created new specialist markets, not all of which are satisfied through health or social services. Provision for infirm elderly people is certainly a growth market in contemporary Britain.

Of course, longevity does not mean that everybody has to look forward to more and more years of infirmity. Assuming that retirement ages do not increase – and we shall see later that the opposite tendency is more likely – we find that more people are reaching retirement in a state of good health, well before the onset of the debilities of old age. Higher standards of living and higher levels of income for the economically active, together with the provision of better pension schemes, both private and state-funded, all mean that people no longer need to work beyond their normal retirement ages. Whereas in 1851 over 80 per cent of men over the age of sixty-five in England and Wales were economically active, by 1971 the figure had fallen to 20 per cent and continues to decline markedly (Joshi 1989: 67). All this means that there is a steadily increasing pro-portion of the population over retirement age, in good health and enjoying economic security, with a wide scope for leisure and recreational activity, ranging from world travel to gardening and increased membership of sports and social clubs. All this gives rise to new and expanding markets for the facilities associated with these activities, and business companies can profitably aim to satisfy such new demand.

Another feature of the growing number of fit people of retirement age is the way in which many of them, though no longer in full-time employ-ment, seek part-time economic activity to supplement their incomes with-out affecting their pension entitlements and to provide continuing interest outside their home lives. Such activity represents a useful contribution to society as a whole, and many businesses will be able to utilize casual employees of this kind, to the benefit of all. In many situations this will involve industrial relations considerations which need to be carefully resolved. But the potential for business growth by employing 'retired' persons should not be ignored.

The fact that retired people are drawing public, private and occupational pensions for more years because of longevity has considerable implications for those pension schemes. Actuarial realities for any pension fund with a growing number of beneficiaries and possibly a declining number of current contributors mean that the funding base needs to be kept under review, with increased contributions from either present employees or from employers. It was noted in Chapter 6 that pension funds figure among the institutional investors who have increasingly come to dominate the stock market, and we now see the importance of those funds in providing regular income for an increasing proportion of the population. The danger of pension funds being misused has implications for both the investment market and for the welfare of pensioners, and the case for more statutory regulation of pension fund management should be closely considered by government.

Earlier retirement

Not only are people living longer beyond retirement age, but there is also a general tendency for reduction in the age of retirement. In some occupations, for instance the army or the police force or the civil service, it has long been the case for the normal retirement age to be below the age of entitlement for the state retirement pension. Furthermore, the ruling by the European courts that equality of opportunity between the sexes requires there to be common retirement ages for men and women will be observed in most cases – but not all – by a lowering of male retirement ages to those of women. In any case, economic and technological trends have in many respects reduced the needs for labour, especially in manufacturing industry. Widespread application of automation has made industry less labour-intensive and, especially in times of economic down-turn, there is less need for labour. Business companies should be able to meet these situations flexibly and imaginatively, with good policies of redundancy and early retirement. With higher levels of wages and salaries than hitherto, the possibilities of job-sharing schemes to offset unemployment need to be carefully considered. All told, however, it is part of modern economic reality that people have neither the need nor the opportunity to spend as high a proportion as hitherto of their lives or of their time each week in economically gainful employment. It is no longer the universal norm that individuals should work on the basis of nine-to-five each day for five days a week right up to the age of sixty-five for men and sixty for women. The money-making part of people's lives need no longer be so predominant as it once was.

Again this has widespread repercussions for other activities. In general people now have more time for leisure, either because they have taken early retirement or because they do not spend the same length of time at work each week. Increased provision of leisure services of all kinds is a feature of the present UK economy which can be expected to remain for the foreseeable future, giving rise to market growth for leisure products and services. Sports for participants and spectators, games, competitions, quizzes and puzzles for individual and group activity, tourism locally, nationally or internationally, gardening, arts and crafts and all manner of do-it-yourself activities are all growth areas in contemporary Britain, and there is substantial potential for business entrepreneurs to use ingenuity and drive to meet the markets in these areas.

The decline in the birth rate

At the same time as the number of older people in the UK has been increasing, so the number of younger people has been declining. After the 'baby boom' of the late 1940s and 1950s, the trend was established by 1975 of an appreciable reduction in the birth rate. The effect of this change was dramatically demonstrated by the fact that, while in 1973 there were over 4.6 million children in maintained primary schools in England, by 1985 the figure had fallen to 3.4 millions (Joshi 1989: 73).

Several factors have contributed to this fall in the birth rate. First, the growing equality of opportunity between men and women in the field of employment opened the possibility for more women to pursue careers, which they did not wish to be interrupted by maternity and the practicalities of raising families. The increasing use of methods of birth control, together with their wider moral acceptability, and the legalizing of abortion in certain circumstances meant that there was more opportunity to avoid unwanted pregnancies and unwanted babies, and the number of births fell. While the post-war 'baby boom' may have been accentuated by the reduced opportunities during the years of the Second World War for new families to be established, so the pendulum may have swung back again in the 1960s as the boom families grew to maturity. While there have been signs since 1980 of a stabilizing in the birth rate it has certainly not reached the proportions of the boom years, and indeed the social trend is increasingly for couples not to be married, or to remain childless while both partners continue in employment. The wish to have a higher standard of living based on two incomes to the household, sometimes described as the 'dinky' phenomenon ('Double Income, No Kids Yet'), has in recent years had a stronger pull for many couples than the natural aspiration to rear a family.

The decline in the birth rate during the 1970s had a dramatic effect on the demand for educational provision, first in the primary schools, where the declining rolls have already been noted, and then in the secondary schools and institutions of further and higher education. We are now in the situation where British universities are increasingly competing to recruit students from the ranks of smaller numbers of school-leavers than for many years. While it is possible for those institutions to lower their entry standards to maintain numbers of students, nothing alters the fact that the number of highly qualified and highly skilled graduates available to enter industry is arguably now lower than a healthy economy would need. Although the present economic recession has made the shortage of graduates less of a problem for industry, the situation remains that industry's longer-term requirement for skilled recruits cannot be met from the present production of graduates, but is met by the retraining of existing employees and the redeployment of others who would be candidates for redundancy in the current economic climate.

While these trends have obvious impact on the recruitment and personnel policies of employing businesses, they also affect the demand for a wide range of products for which young adults are major consumers, particularly new housing and all the items needed in the setting up of new households – furniture, domestic appliances, cutlery and crockery, decorating materials, and so on. Declining demand for such goods may well have been influenced by demographic trends just as much as by economic recession, and manufacturers do well to take that fact into consideration in their production plans.

Equality of opportunity, and mobility of labour

A third, strong demographic trend of recent decades in the UK has been the increase in the number of women in employment. Whereas the historic pattern had been for the great majority of married women to concentrate on their roles as housewives and mothers, the modern trends of women's liberation and equality of opportunity between the sexes have encouraged women to follow careers of their own and to supplement household income by their own earnings. The female percentage of the total workforce in Britain rose from 29.7 per cent in 1931 to 47.0 per cent in 1981, by which date 61.1 per cent of all women aged between twenty and sixty-four were economically active (Joshi 1989: 158). Most of the increase in female employment can be attributed to part-time work, with the percentage of women of the same age-group in part-time employment rising from 5.2 per cent to 27.1 per cent between 1951 and 1981. Part-time work is particularly attractive to women because it can be more easily combined with the domestic activities which are often their responsibility. It is this very large increase in the number of working women which explains what appears at first sight to be a paradox, namely that in recent periods of high unemployment it could still be said that there were more people at work in Britain than ever before.

Several reasons have contributed to this trend towards equal opportunities for women in employment. First, there has been the movement gathering pace throughout this century for women to have more power in British society, with the final acceptance of equal suffrage for women in 1928 leading to more political power for women and the enactment of equal opportunity legislation in the employment field, especially the Equal Pay Act 1970. The role of the Equal Opportunities Commission is now well-established, and many large employers describe themselves as 'equal opportunity employers' in their advertisements of job vacancies. Second, the wider acceptance of contraception and the legalizing of abortion in some circumstances has provided women with more opportunities of breaking out of their traditional domestic moulds, while technological advance has provided more and more labour-saving devices in the home to give women the time to devote to economic activity. Third, the opportunity for women to be employed has supplemented family income and in most cases helped express the aspiration for an increasingly higher material standard of living.

The growth of the number of women in the labour market has far-reaching implications for most businesses. Most obviously, there is the possibility of having more women among the workforce of a business. In most fields, women are now educated and trained to the same levels as men, and recruiting employers are now able to consider female and male applicants on the same merit basis; indeed they are legally required to do so. More generally there are many office and shopfloor activities which seem to suit female labour better than male labour, and it is in these areas that part-time employment and job-sharing opportunities can most easily arise. The employment of women in all these ways is generally to the advantage of most businesses, but it entails sympathetic application of policies of maternity leave and crèche provision.

At the same time, the fact that more women are wage-earners, receiving equal pay for equal work compared with men, means that they have more independent spending-power in the economy, and producers of most goods need to take account of this enhanced role of women as consumers. Advertising, marketing and public relations campaigns need to be directed just as much towards women as men, and products intended for female markets can now enjoy more demand than hitherto. Meanwhile, the advertising of products which can be consumed by both men and women needs increasingly to be angled at the female point of view.

Superimposed on all the national demographic trends which have been described are the regional variations which contribute to different economic patterns from one part of the country to another. The most significant of these variations is the general movement of population from the north and west of Britain to the south and east, with the particularly marked growth of the labour market in 'the broad zone to the north and west of London stretching from Hampshire and Wiltshire through to Cambridgeshire and Norfolk' (Joshi 1989: 115–16) At the same time there has been a dramatic movement of population away from the large cities, especially Greater London, Glasgow, Manchester and Liverpool (Joshi 1989: 121 *et seq.*) into more suburban, rural and new town settings. Modern telecommunications enable more people to work at home or at locations away from city centres, while access to motorways has stimulated population growth along their corridors. Such regional and local demographic variations may give the impression in particular areas that national economic trends do not apply there, while in other places the national picture will be accentuated with harsh severity.

Business companies need to take account of the implications of these regional variations for both their recruitment and marketing policies. While at first sight it may seem sensible to develop new offices and factories in places where there is a ready local labour market, due account has also to be taken of the economics of distribution of products to their markets and of the cost of transport of raw materials and components. In an area of expanding population there are more marketing opportunities, especially in the markets for property and household goods, and businesses may wish to concentrate their advertising strategies on the regional and local media covering those areas. Businesses which supply the national market need constantly to adapt their networks of distribution and market outlets to cater for the changes caused by population growth or decline in different areas.

As the UK becomes more integrated with the rest of the European Community, especially with the creation of a single market throughout the EC, so the horizon for considering demographic trends needs widening to include all member states. Increased mobility of labour within the EC and the opening up of new markets will have implications for all businesses as they face stronger competition from the Continent and seek to benefit from all the new opportunities for trade. Population changes such as have been considered in this chapter now need to be considered on a European scale, for the success of any business depends increasingly on people abroad in the same way as in the home country.

Chapter 9

Business and public relations

WHAT IS PUBLIC RELATIONS?

If running a successful business is all about people, it is desirable that all those people have a good opinion of the business. This involves public relations (PR), the creation and maintenance of good relationships between the business and all sections of its public. And there can be no defined boundaries to that public, for many people who have had no previous contact with a business may be potential future customers, and the opinions of many 'outsiders' may still influence general public opinion about the business. While clearly the relationships between a firm and all its present stakeholders, its employees, shareholders, customers and neighbours, are of immediate importance to the well-being of the business, the image of the firm in the eyes of the public more generally is invariably significant for the business in the longer term. PR is concerned with the relationships between the business and all the public.

PR is different from marketing and advertising, because those activities are essentially related to particular products of a firm and not just to the general image of the firm as a whole. But marketing and advertising are forms of PR because they involve the relationships between the firm and its customers, present and potential. And whereas marketing and advertising are largely within the control of the firm itself, with the form and wording of advertisements deliberately chosen by the firm's own personnel, PR depends much more on what other people say or write about the firm, especially journalists and other opinion formers. Good PR is therefore more valuable than straight advertising, because it either involves testimonials from persons outside the firm, or allows facts to speak for themselves. And PR items are generally less costly than advertising, with all its expensive insertion rates. On the other hand, good PR calls for a great deal more trouble by the firm's personnel over a long period of time in developing public awareness and goodwill.

Effective PR on a continuing basis really requires the appointment of specific public relations officers (PROs) on the permanent pay-roll of the business. While small firms may be in no position to afford a permanent PRO, their managing directors or other general managers may find it advisable to take responsibility themselves for the firm's PR work, rather than hiring outside consultants. While there are many PR consultancies available for hire nowadays, their services are generally expensive, and they cannot possibly have the same experience and knowledge of the firm's activities as permanent personnel. All outside PR consultants need very full briefing by internal staff, whose time might more profitably have been spent in direct contact with the news media or local opinion formers. Members of the press and public are bound to have much more confidence if they are dealing direct with staff internal to an organization, rather than at arm's length with third parties external to the organization itself. But any in-house PRO needs to have authority and easy means of communication within the firm itself in order to find out what is happening in all departments, so he or she needs to occupy a place high in the firm's hierarchy and to report directly to the managing director. If there is no PRO in the company with a seat on the board as Director of Public Relations, then the senior PRO should generally be able to attend board meetings, without a vote, in order to advise on the PR aspects of any items of business and to know what is happening throughout the company. A good, close working relationship between the managing director and the firm's senior PRO is essential for the maintenance of good PR.

RELATIONS WITH THE NEWS MEDIA

Almost certainly the most effective and most used channel for PR is through the news media, newspapers, journals, magazines, radio and television, with all their outlets to the general public. Whether a firm likes it or not, these organs of information will almost certainly convey news about the firm to their readers and viewers, and it is therefore essential that good relations be established with their appropriate personnel. Some journalists and broadcasters will act as opinion-leaders in relation to the firm's activities and products, and they need to be cultivated and kept informed of news from the business. More importantly, the news media can be utilized by any efficient PRO to gain valuable coverage for items of news about the firm, and that PRO will need to have a continuing rapport with news reporters.

At the outset of establishing PR for a firm, a full list needs to be drawn up of all the news organizations which have access to the firm's public, and of the appropriate reporters within those organizations with whom the firm should liaise. These organizations will include local and regional newspapers and free broadsheets circulating in the locality of the firm's premises, any freelance or national journalists living in the area, trade journals and specialist magazines, local radio and regional television stations. Attempts should be made to establish contact with key reporters from these organizations, either by making appointments to see them at their offices or by inviting them to visit the firm's premises for a general briefing, for a tour of the site and for limited hospitality, which should neither be lavish nor stinted, but appropriate to the occasion. These contacts will not necessarily be themselves newsworthy, but the interest of journalists will be increased if they can be combined with the announcement of some important news item concerning the firm's activities. Unless there is some such specific item of news to announce, it will almost certainly be more appropriate to meet journalists one at a time, for they are all competitors of each other and will not take kindly to being lumped together.

Having established an initial contact with news media personnel, it is important to nourish those links by providing them with newsworthy items as often as they are available, and hopefully at least once every three months. When contacts go cold by less frequent contact, the initial effort in establishing them is wasted. In supplying items to news reporters, care should be taken in relation to closing times for copy to local newspapers, for if the week's deadline has just been missed it is unlikely that the item will be carried the following week, especially if the same news has already appeared in a rival newspaper. There is great rivalry between newspapers for being first with the news, especially in the same local area.

At the same time, discrimination needs to be shown in deciding what items to send to news media. Many items which may appear very interesting within a firm, such as the publication of an annual report or the achievement of record production or sales levels, may well go down like lead balloons with journalists and broadcasters, and there is danger in becoming known in the media as a firm whose news is never interesting. The key factor in determining the newsworthiness of any item is whether it carries human interest, which will enable readers and viewers to identify with the circumstances described. In addition, items for local news media should always carry local interest; sometimes this will apply automatically because the item concerns the local premises or personnel of the firm, but local journalists are hardly likely to respond enthusiastically to a press extract of the local general manager's speech about the state of the national economy!

Newsworthy items do not generally arise to order, and an effective PRO must constantly be on the alert to recognize those items arising in the normal course of a firm's activities which will be of interest to the media. Gimmicks to create news artificially are not generally well-received by the media. While PROs need to be assiduous in nosing out items of real news and interest from within the firm, they also have to exercise patience and some ruthlessness in deciding not to send news reporters items which will clearly not arouse interest.

The traditional means of sending news items to news reporters is through the written press release; only in very exceptional circumstances, such as when a local newspaper's deadline is imminent, should a news item be telephoned to a reporter, for mistakes and misunderstandings can then so easily occur and the reporter has less opportunity to put the item together as he or she would wish. But in composing press releases, PROs need to take care to observe several invariable rules. First and foremost, the press release should never cover more than one side of A4 paper; if the item is too long to be included on one side, then it will almost certainly be too long to be included in any news report, and it will always be too long for any reporter to read as he wades through his pile of morning post. The script of the press release needs to be set out in double-spacing and with generous margins so that the reporter can add his or her own notes. It is wise to put a title to the press release to encapsulate the whole significance of the item; such a title needs to be designed to capture the interest of the reporter, and should not aim to be the title for the eventual printed report, for the wording of that is always the prerogative of the sub-editor, who will be more concerned with fitting in the wording to the space available, rather than conveying any message. The first paragraph of the press release should summarize the whole news item; if the reporter has not been able to see the full significance of the release in that first paragraph, it may well be assigned to the waste-paper basket. Consequently, the second and any subsequent paragraphs should include comments of secondary interest with which the reporter can expand the article if he or she wishes.

Moreover, it is often good tactics to keep some such secondary piece of information out of the release itself, so that there can be something extra to reveal to any interested reporter who, after receiving the release, then telephones to seek an additional and particular angle on the story. Every release should include, either at the top or the bottom, the name, address and telephone number for further contact. If a reporter does respond by making such contact, you can be sure that interest in the news item has been aroused and that some media coverage will result. It is wise to co-operate with a further inquiry in this way, and the provision of further information will build up the confidence of the reporter for future work.

At the same time, there are a few things which should never be done in connection with a press release. Never include long enclosures with a release, for they can only serve to undermine its pithiness. Never include photographs, for news media who wish to use photographs will almost certainly wish to make their own arrangements for taking them. Never include samples of products, for they simply clutter up the desk of the reporter and can sometimes appear to be small bribes. And, if possible, it is wise to avoid putting a time embargo on the press release, for that will only serve to irritate journalists who need, or wish, to be off the mark immediately, and in any case it may not be observed and carries no power of enforcement. Finally, no press release should contain material which the firm itself does not wish to be divulged publicly, for reasons of commercial confidentiality or security. Often a PRO needs to be very careful in checking with the managing director that the information contained in a press release is what the firm really wishes to make public. Again in this context it helps if the PRO is a member of the firm's own staff.

All these considerations about press releases apply whatever the news medium, whether it be press, radio or television, and local, regional or national. An additional factor for releases to local media must always be that their material must emphasize the local aspects of the story; without such aspects the release will almost certainly be passed over without interest. While the use of a press release on radio or television is itself a measure of PR success because of the wider public reached and the greater impact of something which is heard or seen, rather than read, there is always the possibility that interest in the broadcasting media may lead to some interview of a representative from the business to be broadcast, either recorded or live, either in the studio or on location. Whoever appears to represent a firm in such a broadcast interview is advised to undergo some form of prior training, if only in a thorough discussion with the PRO. Broadcasting requires special skills, and there are special seminars and short courses, usually involving practice interviews, which can greatly assist the general business executive before agreeing to participate in a broadcast interview.

Of course, PR is a two-way process and no business organization is able always to control the subject matter being considered in its contacts with the media. Whether a firm has taken trouble to cultivate good PR contacts or not, there will still be occasions when a news organization somehow receives information which the firm would not necessarily wish to be made public. A journalist will in these circumstances contact the firm for more information and comments. This need not be the same journalist that the PRO has been cultivating assiduously in the same media organization, and the journalist may well go about the inquiry with hostility and rudeness. The one point that is fairly certain in these circumstances is that the journalist is already interested in the subject-matter of the inquiry, so that there will be some coverage of the issue in the media. It is pointless to try to persuade the journalist to drop the issue, because such an attempt will almost certainly arouse the suspicion of the reporter that there is something which the firm wishes to hide.

Similarly, only harm can result from a 'No comment' response: any report which appears subsequently would almost certainly state that the firm's spokesman had no comment to make, which gives the appearance that the firm has no defence to offer to any criticisms, and may also appear very rude. In dealing with any reporter's unexpected telephone inquiry, the best policy is to remain calm and courteous and to go out of one's way to be helpful. It is very often the case that the person receiving the call has no knowledge of the matter to which the inquiry relates, or only partial knowledge, or may not be sure about what the firm would wish to be publicly divulged. In those circumstances it is reasonable to ask the caller to spell out how he or she would like your assistance and then to indicate that you need a short time to make further inquiries, but that you will telephone back to the same reporter with a full response. To do this, it is necessary to note the name and telephone number of the caller, and to ascertain whether he or she will still be available during the next half-hour during which you intend to return the call. Above everything else, make sure that you do ring back within that time: not only will you have a prepared statement to give, but you will also be more fully briefed about the problem and better able to answer further points. Failure to ring back is as bad as using the 'No comment' formula. One very bad PR practice once employed by one firm was to refer all telephone inquiries from the media to an unmanned telephone which was never answered; eventually the firm realized why they received only bad press coverage!

In order to gauge the PR impact of any press release or media interview, it is vital to monitor the media, to build up a record of press cuttings and videotape or audiocassette recordings of relevant television and radio broadcasts. With regard to newspapers and magazines, it is possible for the PR office in a firm to subscribe to publications on a regular basis and for a member of staff to scan the pages for all items of relevance to the firm; for very local newspapers this is the surest way of monitoring coverage thoroughly and quickly. More generally, it is good policy to use the services of a cuttings agency to provide cuttings of all articles which mention the firm, for these will include many which are not circulated in the immediate neighbourhood of the business and many of which there was no warning prior to publication. The PRO needs to see every public comment about his firm. With regard to radio and television, it is not so easy to be sure of recording all broadcast items relating to a firm: the most practical method is to employ the services of a housewife or pensioner to monitor local radio and television channels, particularly news programmes, in order to keep a record of any relevant items. This can be a time-consuming exercise, however, and the outcome may not merit the trouble involved. When broadcast items do refer to a firm, it is always possible for the firm subsequently to request from the station controller a copy of the transcript or even of a videotape, but this depends on knowing when the item was broadcast.

While most PR work involves good relations with the news media and will produce good coverage for a business, it must be remembered that the news media are independent agencies, beholden to none of their suppliers of news. In practice the only items a newspaper is bound to print are adjudications of the Press Council relating to that newspaper or, for legal reasons, retractions or apologies arising from earlier articles. Otherwise a local newspaper may refuse to report any category of news which it wishes, for instance all political news, and nobody else can do anything about it. Furthermore, the news media have remarkably wide licence to print whatever they wish, and are answerable only to the courts in respect of charges of defamation and to the Press Council in respect of complaints made to that body. Otherwise newspapers are not accountable for what they print, no matter how much impact it might have. They have power without responsibility, a circumstance described by the writer Rudyard Kipling, quoted by his cousin prime minister Stanley Baldwin, as 'the prerogative of the harlot through the centuries'. Businesses, in common with other individuals and organizations, may often feel dissatisfied with press coverage of their activities, and may wonder whether to seek redress and how to do so.

Any legal action or official complaint against a newspaper should be taken only very much as a last resort in circumstances which require action but no other action is possible. Several caveats are necessary here. First, while the publicity given to the firm may not have been desirable or fair or even accurate, it was publicity all the same, and there is a school of thought which claims that even bad publicity is better than no publicity. Even when it is considered that some bad publicity will be detrimental to the company's interests, the company should consider carefully whether those interests might be more seriously harmed by the loss of media goodwill that would result from the making of an official complaint, even if that complaint is found to have been justified. If much time and trouble have already been taken in building up goodwill with the news organization concerned, its effects could all be destroyed by taking the editor to court or reporting him or her to the Press Council. Far more effective, and in the long run more satisfactory, is to make an informal approach to the journalist concerned, or if necessary to the editor, and air the grievance in a friendly way in the hope that the matter can be discussed reasonably. While this may not lead to a printed apology or retraction, it can bring about a better working relationship in future; the interests of the firm are not harmed when reporters are aware that the results of their work are being carefully scrutinized by the firm.

When an informal complaint is completely rejected by a newspaper editor, and the firm continues to feel a real grievance that its business interests may have been harmed, a very careful exercise needs to be undertaken before deciding on any further action. Whether to complain to the Press Council – or in the case of broadcasting to the broadcasting complaints bodies – or to take legal action will depend upon the circumstances involved. In the former case the procedure is not expensive but may lead to a permanent loss of goodwill with the media organization involved, which may well be worse than any temporary loss of business due to the offending article. Legal action can be very expensive and, even if successful, will lose the goodwill of the defendant and almost certainly of other news organizations, who will be very wary in any future contacts with the firm. In some cases, legal action would not be advisable because it would almost certainly fail. In short, complaining to the Press Council or to the courts is an admission of PR failure, and there are other ways of overcoming the difficulties which have given rise to the complaint. It has to be remembered that news media organizations are made up of human beings, who are all fallible and who generally wish to get on well with those with whom they have regular contact; furthermore news organizations are themselves businesses which need good PR, and it is unusual for them, especially at local level, to wish to antagonize any influential part of the community.

RELATIONS WITH STAKEHOLDERS

While the news media can be helpful to a business in establishing good PR throughout a whole community, at local, regional or national level, they have only an indirect effect on the specific relations between a firm and its stakeholders, namely its employees, shareholders, customers or local neighbours. More direct methods need to be used towards them.

For personnel employed by the firm, the key means of communication is an in-house magazine or news-sheet delivered on a regular basis to all staff, whether salaried or wage-earning. This publication will seek to inform employees of most news about the company and its operations, to report any interesting activities of staff, either in the course of their work or not, and to provide a platform for members of staff themselves to air their views about the way the company is run. All successful PR is a two-way process, and it is wrong to limit an in-house publication to statements of official policy or to adulation of members of the board! When an in-house publication has been in existence for some time, it is useful to conduct a survey of employees' unattributed views about it, to see how it might be improved. Other activities to establish good rapport between a firm and its staff may include the organization of summer outings or Christmas parties and carol services, of sports and entertainment programmes, and encouraging staff to form their own interest groups and societies. These and many other examples increase employees' sense of belonging to the firm and of having a stake in its well-being. More importantly, the attitudes of staff towards the firm can be influenced by overall employment policies, such as contract terms in respect of sickness pay, maternity leave, pensions, redundancy, participation in share-owner-ship schemes, and so on. Human relationships at work all contribute to the total PR programme of the business.

Similarly, another constituent part of a firm's public is made up of the shareholders, who have provided a major part of the capital by which the business has been developed. While in money terms the largest share-holders will be institutions of the kinds described in Chapter 6, there will still be very large numbers of individual shareholders, particularly in the newly-privatized businesses, and the well-being of the company depends on their goodwill. If some policy or attitude of the company antagonizes a large number of shareholders, they may be tempted to dispose of their holdings, with the result that the share price may decline and general financial confidence in the business be undermined. The one occasion each year when shareholders have a right to be involved directly in the affairs of a company is at the annual general meeting, and much can be done in PR terms to make that an interesting, informative and constructive occasion for shareholders. Questions raised by shareholders in the meeting should be given full answers, with the admission of mistakes where appro-priate. Promises to investigate any individual complaints should be hon-oured, with appropriate reports back to the shareholders raising them. At other times of the year it may be thought helpful for the company chair-man to send a letter over his signature to all shareholders to explain some new policy initiative, or the company's attitude on an issue of public interest. Such communication will help to substantiate shareholders' sense of identity with the company. So also will the provision of small perqui-sites, such as concessionary use of company facilities. If those facilities are currently under-used, provision of the concession will not cost the com-pany a large amount, and that cost will be more than offset by the goodwill that results.

The third group of stakeholders whose goodwill is vital to any business are the customers, present and future. Product advertising and marketing are really PR campaigns to win the goodwill of customers in the purchase of goods. Much can then be done in the process of the sale to retain the goodwill of each customer. Most important is the reliability and durability of the product itself, for there is nothing more likely to destroy customer goodwill than the early failure of a product. Arrangements for guaranteeing and replacing faulty products are also important to the customer, as is the whole 'after-market' for servicing and repair. If customers find they can never get spare parts for their goods, or if they have to throw the whole thing away as soon as it goes wrong in the slightest respect, or if the network of retailers is geographically sparse, those customers are unlikely to purchase another product from the same company. Similarly, the good-will of customers can be jeopardized if the packaging of products is difficult to open or disguises the small quantity of product per package, or if the wording of instructions relevant to the product is not clear. Customer relations departments of firms need to deal with all enquiries and complaints sympathetically, with promises to consider all suggestions fully; too many replies from such departments seem to be standard letters avoiding the whole point which the customer has made. Cosmetic customer relations, like all cosmetic PR, is almost worse than no PR at all, because it creates frustration, irritation and antagonism towards the company.

Finally, there are the local residents in the community or communities where the company has its premises, some of them close neighbours whose homes are adjacent to the company's property. Their goodwill can be very important for the company in crisis situations, such as are considered in the next section, or in relation to political decisions and public authorities, for example in determining planning applications or enforcing pollution controls. It can be helpful for regular liaison to be maintained between the firm and representatives of the local community, possibly through local councillors, and it is good policy to keep local residents informed by letter of any changes in company operations which would affect them in any way. The PR department at the company's premises should maintain an open door to receive complaints and inquiries from local residents, and it is good PR to hold open days on the premises when local residents and the families of staff are able to tour the site and enjoy entertainment of various kinds. In addition, many firms sponsor local charities and community facilities or events, and allow their own premises, where appropriate, to be used by community organizations. The standing of the firm in the eyes of the local community can be much enhanced by these means, so that it becomes easier to recruit local labour and maintain co-operation with local residents when problem situations arise.

All these methods of fostering good relations between a business and its stakeholders are aspects of general PR. They also demonstrate once more the value of PR work being the responsibility of full-time employees of the company; only then can there be regular and uninhibited access to employee relations personnel, customer relations departments and to finance departments who liaise with shareholders. Public relations involves an integrated approach, embracing the whole life of a business, and it is very difficult for this to be done satisfactorily by agencies which are outside the business.

CRISIS MANAGEMENT

Every business is likely to face a crisis situation at some time or other, whether it be due to an industrial relations dispute, a physical disaster like a fire or an explosion, a need to recall products, a financial crisis on the Stock Exchange, or a take-over bid. It is in such times of crisis that the firm will need to draw on the reservoir of goodwill built up by careful PR over the years. Any crisis calls for considerable PR activity; the firm is likely to be the focus of major public attention and scrutiny, with the news media clamouring to know what is happening, with the staff and local community anxious to know whether jobs at the firm are safe for the future, and with confidence among shareholders in a sensitive state. In the nature of things, most crises are unforeseen, and most firms need to react to them on the spur of the moment. However, it is not impossible to do some contingency planning for crisis situations, and any firm is wise to have such plans in readiness. (*vide* Jefkins 1987: chapter 19)

The basic response of crisis planning is to set up a small crisis management team within the firm, consisting of not more than four or five people, possibly including the managing director, the local PRO, the local personnel manager, a safety officer with full technical knowledge of local operations, and a financial director. This team should at the outset draw up a list of all the possible crises that could be imagined as happening to the firm, and dividing the list into categories of likelihood. Each of these potential crises needs to be discussed by the team, giving more, but not exclusive, attention to the more likely ones, and a draft of contingency plans needs to be made for each, including lists of people who need to be contacted immediately in such an emergency. If a physical disaster were to engulf the premises of the firm, the team would need an alternative location to meet nearby, in order to direct operations. The members of the team should all carry lists of telephone numbers at which all the other members of the team can be contacted around the clock, and most of the team need to have substitutes, if possible, in case they are themselves unavailable when a crisis occurs. This crisis management team needs to meet at regular intervals, say once every three months, to keep its plans under review, especially to think of all the things that could go wrong with the contingency plans themselves, such as loss of all telephone communication.

If, unfortunately, a crisis does occur, the firm should aim to be as open as possible in all dealings with the public and the news media. Sometimes crises can be turned to good PR advantage, for instance in going to great lengths, such as placing public advertisements, to recall products which have been found faulty. If the business is seen to operate openly in this way, taking positive steps to rectify a problem, public confidence will be damaged much less than would have been the case if the firm had pretended that no problem existed, or had reacted to it with great secrecy.

Some crises, such as leaks of gas or poisonous substances, or spillages of oil, involve environmental damage, and the next chapter will consider in more detail all the ways in which the activities of a business have an impact on the physical environment.

Chapter 10

Business and the physical environment

THE NEED FOR ENVIRONMENTAL AWARENESS

Until the 1950s few businessmen and industrialists were concerned about the impact of their activities on the physical environment. Many places of work, particularly in heavy industry, were exceedingly dirty, with noxious effluent pouring into nearby water-courses and black smoke belching from many chimneys. The existence of filthy surroundings was accepted as an almost inevitable consequence of much economic activity, summed up in the north country saying, 'Where there's muck, there's brass.' In many industrial areas, the air was laden with dirt, covering washing hung out to dry and filling people's nostrils as they breathed. Towns were often subject to low-lying fog and poisonous smog, responsible for the deaths of many thousands and chronic illnesses for far more. Railway journeys were dirty experiences, and passengers could easily be covered in smuts emitted from the funnels of steam locomotives.

Thankfully, this has all changed in the last forty years. All businesses now need to take account of the impact of their operations on the physical environment. One reason for this concern is because the law requires it. The smogs of the 1950s were ended by smoke control legislation applied by local authorities throughout the country, with the extension of clean air zones to cover most built-up areas. The Control of Pollution Act of 1974 codified much previous legislation in this field and introduced new powers to prevent toxic emissions of gas and liquid from industrial premises. The Alkali Inspectorate was integrated with the new Health and Safety Executive. Further consolidation and extension of powers to control pollution was effected by the Environmental Protection Act of 1990, to be implemented and enforced by local authorities and by HM Inspectorate of Pollution. Firms which fail to observe all these statutory controls are liable to legal penalties imposed by the courts, besides any resulting bad publicity.

The growth of statute law in this field has come about through political pressures and through developments in public opinion which have made people everywhere more aware of environmental considerations. With the extension of education and the spread of knowledge by the mass media, people have become much more aware of the damage that pollution can cause to health and of the dangers for children and animals; they have also become more critical of the aesthetic impact of pollution on their whole environment. People today want to live in pleasant areas free from smoke and fumes, smells and polluted water. Furthermore, public opinion has come to realize the wider damage done to the world's environment by industrial pollution, such as the way emissions of sulphur dioxide lead to acid rain and the killing of forests and wildlife, or how deforestation contributes to flooding disasters, or how the burning of fossil fuels and timber contributes to global warming and the possible raising of sea level. The influence of green pressure groups in many advanced countries has extended environmental awareness among the general public, so that more and more people take steps to recycle wastepaper and bottles, or avoid using aerosol sprays which might have a damaging effect on the world's ozone layer, or avoid buying products made from limited, non-renewable resources. Some companies, such as the Body Shop, have built up commercial success by supplying only 'environmentally friendly' products, and many firms have amended their policies to cater for the 'green' market. There is no doubt that the present ethos of public opinion in the western world includes an expanding green element, and successful businesses need to take account of that if they are to survive and flourish.

The ethical considerations of Chapter 5 take the green issue further for business companies. Not only should firms take account of the climate of public opinion in the community where they operate, but they should also see that it is wrong in terms of absolute principle to damage the environment, or to produce goods which may have a harmful effect on people's health, or to deplete scarce natural resources. Not only will firms jeopardize their own futures if they help to exhaust supplies of essential raw materials or to supply harmful goods, they will also be acting wrongly in absolute terms. All three branches of ethics, the transcendental, the social and the utilitarian, combine to impel any successful business to pursue environmentally friendly policies. This whole case was recently well expounded by Pearce (1991). In the remainder of this chapter, consideration is given to the particular impacts of environmental considerations on manufacturing processes and on the nature of the goods supplied to the market.

THE ENVIRONMENT AND INDUSTRIAL PROCESSES

Every stage of an industrial process involves environmental considerations. Some of these may run counter to commercial considerations, but others may not. First, there is the important choice of raw materials for any process. When raw materials are in limited supply, this will usually be reflected in their price, and then commercial and environmental considerations will be in agreement. Sometimes, however, a commodity may seem reasonably plentiful, but its use may be environmentally detrimental, such as timber from the tropical rain forests, and then either other timber or an alternative resource should be used. All opportunities for using recycled raw materials should be fully explored. For many years, glass manufacturers maintained that it was not technically appropriate to melt down glass bottles for use in producing new ones, but further research enabled methods to be found for doing this very successfully. Recycling of any commodity has two environmental advantages, namely the conservation of raw materials and the avoidance of having to find space or other means to dispose of used items.

The choice of raw materials will usually involve consideration of how those materials are transported to the manufacturing site. If many lorry-loads of the material are required, on a continual basis, road transport may add to all the pollution problems of heavily congested roads, or may involve the use of unsuitable roads in residential areas. Spillage of material from lorries can cause horrendous environmental problems. If alternative means or routes for transport cannot be found, then consideration should be given to using other raw materials.

Similar considerations can be applied in the choice of fuel used in any manufacturing process. The use of coal or coke will usually produce environmentally undesirable smoke and ash, and will entail all the problems of transporting the fuel to the site. Transport problems also arise in most uses of oil as a fuel rather than as a feedstock, in which case pipeline supply may be possible. Natural gas is relatively clean and easy to supply by pipe, but there is only a finite supply. The fuel which is both clean and easy to supply, and which, as a secondary fuel, is itself not faced with possible depletion, is electricity. Companies faced with a choice of fuels should weigh up all these and similar considerations.

Businesses should consider the potential dangers arising from their manufacturing processes, both within the workplace itself with possible hazards for employees, and also for the surrounding district. The explosion at the Flixborough chemical works near Scunthorpe in 1974, the Bhopal disaster in India in 1984 and the Chernobyl meltdown at a nuclear power station in the Ukraine in 1986 have shown the world the potentially lethal nature of some industrial processes for people living over wide areas; other manufacturing plant may entail risk to smaller areas but with similar levels of danger and environmental damage. Businesses need to take all possible steps to reduce levels of risk, and in some cases to explore the possibility of alternative processes which are less hazardous.

Most industrial processes involve waste material which needs disposing of, whether in solid, liquid or gaseous form. The problems of waste disposal from industrial premises are perhaps the most difficult of all environmental problems. Solid wastes may take up valuable land space, and their transportation may give rise to a host of other environmental problems. For example, slurry from colliery washing plants or fly ash from power stations present vile problems for local residents in roads along which they may be transported by lorry. Liquids poured into streams, rivers or the sea may kill fish or vegetation or have all kinds of other undesirable effects. For example, effluent from one chemical works resulted in the deposition of sodium chlorate along the banks of a local stream along which residents were accustomed to take their dogs for walks. As sodium chlorate is well-known as an animal laxative, not much imagination is required to picture the mess that followed! The image of that firm in some local eyes was not good for some time. And gases which escape from industrial processes via chimneys may cause environmental problems locally as well as much further afield, with powders deposited over the surrounding area, harming property and gardens and possibly injuring health. Attempts to dispose of toxic or noxious substances at sea are fraught with difficulties of transportation and questions about the durability of storage containers.

While the problems of waste disposal will vary according to the process which produces them, managers need to consider whether processes can be altered to produce less waste, or whether additional stages can be introduced to render waste non-toxic and less harmful. If there is no way of avoiding noxious waste substances, then special measures need to be taken for transporting them away, preferably by pipeline, for safe disposal where they can never cause any harm. This is much more easily said than done. If waste disposal problems are insuperable, the firm may prefer to change to manufacturing other products.

Products and the environment

In the same way as most manufacturing processes have an impact on the environment, so the products from them – and the ways they are distributed and packaged – may have harmful environmental effects. Managers need to consider how such harm can be minimized by product substitution or amendment and by alternative means of distribution and packing.

First, there are some commodities which cause environmental damage simply through being used. For example, leaded petrol pollutes the atmosphere when it is used. Some soaps, detergents and washing-up liquids are non-biodegradable, with the result that they produce large amounts of foam when they are poured down drains and flow into rivers. Plain white toilet paper dissolves more easily than paper dyed a different colour. Some agricultural fertilizers are washed through the soil into water-bearing rocks underneath, where they may contaminate public water supplies and have injurious effects on public health. In all such cases, damage to the environment can be reduced or avoided by the supply or use of alternative products. The government has taken a lead by reducing petrol tax on unleaded petrol; manufacturers might also encourage the use of more environmentally friendly alternative products by suitable price differentials.

Many commodities cause immense environmental damage when they need disposal. Scrap-metal yards take up large acreages of land and are horrendous eyesores, with their heaps of mangled cars and domestic appliances. The throw-away economy, with many goods becoming rapidly obsolete and impossible to repair when they develop any small fault, has caused vast environmental harm. Rubber tyres which have exhausted their usefulness, even as retreads, either occupy large sites or, when burnt, cause thick, noxious fumes. Whenever disposal of a commodity is difficult, the original manufacturers need to consider whether the product can be amended to make disposal easier, or whether better repair and maintenance facilities can be introduced to extend the useful lifetime of the product, and what opportunities there are for recycling the product, as a whole or in part, to make disposal unnecessary. Future generations need to be spared the legacy of a throw-away society.

The packaging of many commodities may also cause environmental problems. Mention has already been made of the possible effect of aerosol spray cans, with their CFC gases, on the earth's ozone layer. There are also many types of plastic container which are impossible to destroy when they have been used; polystyrene packing material is bulky and difficult to discard. In all such instances, manufacturers should consider what alternative packaging materials are available, and what opportunities there are for recycling containers, as has been done with much success in respect of glass bottles. If containers cannot be filled again with the same product as before, then at least it may be possible to use them in the manufacture of fresh containers.

The appearance of premises

Another important part of the environmental impact of a business is the appearance and design of its premises, whether these are factories, offices, depots or warehouses. In the nineteenth century, the era of Blake's 'dark satanic mills', very little thought was given to the visual impact of industrial and commercial premises, and the landscape in industrial areas was generally dominated by tall chimneys, blast furnaces, coke ovens, pit winding-gear and slag heaps. William Lever's development at Port Sunlight was revolutionary for its time. A century later there is far more opportunity for business and industrial premises to be designed and constructed as pleasant places to see and visit, and to fit in with the surrounding landscape. The use of electricity as the basic fuel in factories helps to keep them clean, without the need for tall chimneys. Modern architecture enables the design of premises to be both functional and to blend better with the environment, as for example with the boxing-in of the winding-gear of modern collieries. All such improvement of the appearance of industrial and commercial premises is good from an environmental standpoint; it helps to attract staff and business customers, and it improves the public image of the business as a whole.

Chapter 11

Conclusion

Each of the foregoing chapters has opened a new window through which the business manager is able to view the surrounding community and to take account of the interactions between the community and his or her business. The view through each window has been described in very general terms, and indeed a complete book would be necessary in each case to give a fully detailed picture. The interested reader will no doubt be able to find more specialized works on each topic if a more detailed study is required. This work has been designed simply to give an overall introduction to the whole field of Management and Society, and to provide the overview which many present and potential future managers need. And each view described has concentrated mainly on the UK scene, for that is where the author's experience has been concentrated and where the need for this book has arisen. While the growing involvement of the UK in the European Community has necessitated the inclusion in Chapter 3 of some description of the impact of the Community on UK businesses, and while the UK scene is reflected in many respects in other countries around the world, particularly within the Commonwealth, the international dimension to British business has in general not been explored here.

Indeed, international business is increasingly a whole subject in its own right within postgraduate MBA courses, with many facets. International trade involves many practical and technical problems of its own, concerning import and export arrangements, currency exchange and taxation implications, particularly for multinational corporations. The ramifications of international politics cause many complications for trading overseas. The relationship between international trade and the need for development assistance for less developed countries is another whole subject in its own right. The recent changes in Eastern Europe and the former Soviet Union, with the ending of their controlled economies, have opened up new markets for UK exports with new problems for British traders. And the field of international finance and investment, including the relationships between stock exchanges around the world, calls for highly specialized study drawing on expert knowledge. There are many international windows, therefore, which remained unopened in this book; that is not to diminish their importance, and the reader is referred to the ever-expanding literature on international business for more information on these matters.

Similarly, there has been only passing mention in this book of the whole field of human resource management and industrial relations. This is partly because this area of business management is largely internal to business company activities, although of course trade unions are themselves external organizations. More importantly, human resource management is increasingly a subject in its own right in postgraduate programmes and does not fit easily as a small component of a Management and Society syllabus. Again there is considerable literature in this field for the interested reader. And in the same way, the topics of marketing and advertising, while certainly forming part of the relationship between a business and the wider community, are subjects in their own right within management programmes, having their own literature.

Business management calls for expertise covering many disciplines, and the whole approach of the successful manager must include the ability to relate many diverse topics to one another and to co-ordinate teams made up of experts in different disciplines. The art of good management depends in the first instance more on an attitude of mind than on competence in applying the minutiae of many areas of knowledge. That attitude of mind needs to be holistic, with the ability to see the whole wood and not just individual trees, and involves constantly monitoring all new developments outside, judging with the benefit of experience how best the business can be organized to take account of those developments. If this book has helped to foster that attitude of mind among present and future managers, it will have served its purpose.

Appendix I

The business ethics game (BEG)

This game requires at least two players. First each player independently writes out the code of ethics which he or she would aim to apply in the context of general business activity, and identifies the code by appending his or her name. These codes should be written before reading through the case studies set out on the following pages. At no stage should any player seek to explain or amplify his or her code orally to anyone else. Codes are then exchanged, and those who receive them are forbidden to ask any questions about them of their original authors.

Using the written code which they have received, each player then works through the following ten case studies. In each case there are two decisions to be reached: first, the decision which most closely arises from the written code which the player is following; and second, the decision which the player would have taken himself or herself. The player then completes the first column – and only the first column – of a copy of the summary chart which appears after the case studies, and returns that copy of the chart, together with the written code of ethics which he or she has been following, to the original author of that code. Every player having received back his own code of ethics, together with the partially completed summary chart, should then fill in the remaining sections of the chart, and work out the correspondence between his or her own decisions and those of the person who used the player's written code.

Of course, some measure of agreement between the two sets of decisions could occur by chance, and it can be shown mathematically that the most probable final score arising from such chance agreements is 34 per cent. For decisions to have been aided by the written code of ethics, the player's final score must therefore exceed that chance score.

This business ethics game is based on an idea developed by Scott Armstrong in his Ideal Manager Exercise, but all the cases listed below are entirely new. The purpose of the game is to demonstrate the difficulty of expressing a code of ethics with the clarity to suit all manner of circumstances. After the game has been played, individual players may wish to make another attempt at writing their codes of ethics.

CASE 1: THE CRIMINALS

You have discovered that a group of your superiors at work are involved in a business practice which you are convinced is criminally illegal. Do you:

(a) do nothing,
(b) take up the issue with one of the persons concerned,
(c) report the situation to a manager senior to those concerned,
(d) report the matter anonymously to the police, or
(e) seek the earliest opportunity to leave the organization?

Decision arising from the written code . . .
Your own decision . . .

CASE 2: THE APPLICANT

An acquaintance of yours, who you know has in the past been convicted of theft, is being considered for a responsible post with the firm where you work. There has been no requirement for the applicant to divulge this criminal record in making the application for employment. Do you:

(a) do nothing,
(b) take up the matter with the applicant, pressing him or her to divulge the criminal record, or
(c) report the information to the appropriate manager in the firm?

Decision arising from the written code . . .
Your own decision . . .

CASE 3: THE FIRE

A company of which you are director has decided to demolish some buildings owned by the company and redevelop the site, but this decision has not been made public and is known only to very few people within the company. By chance, the buildings are totally destroyed by fire a few days later. Do you:

(a) support a decision to make an insurance claim for fire damage loss, or
(b) not?

Decision arising from the written code . . .
Your own decision . . .

CASE 4: THE DRUG

As director of a drug company, you are aware that one of the company's products is thought to have detrimental side effects when taken by pregnant women, which could cause disabilities in their future children. On the other hand, there is no known substitute for the drug in helping to cure the condition for which it has been produced and marketed. In your discussions with fellow-directors on this matter, do you advocate:

(a) no change in the company's practice in marketing the drug,
(b) withdrawal of the drug from the market, or
(c) the inclusion of an appropriate warning in all literature advertising the drug or accompanying supplies of it?

Decision arising from the written code . . .
You own decision . . .

CASE 5: CONFIDENTIALITY

You have recently changed jobs from one chemical company to another. Although the two companies produce different chemicals for different markets, you are surprised to find that one of the problems you are asked to work on by your new employer is very similar to a problem you had successfully resolved in the previous company. The detailed method which you had used in solving that problem is not known publicly, and must be regarded as commercially confidential to your previous employers. Do you:

(a) go ahead and use the confidential information which you possess in solving your new employer's problem,
(b) ask to be transferred to other work within your new company, or
(c) explain your dilemma to your new superior, and agree to follow his guidance in the situation?

Decision arising from the written code . . .
Your own decision . . .

CASE 6: THE AFFAIR

You are a young, unmarried employee in a large organization, and your immediate superior – with whom you have a good relationship – is a married person of the same sex as you. You are surprised and flattered to receive amorous attention from your superior's attractive spouse, and you enjoy the developing affair, although you feel intensely guilty of disloyalty to your superior. In due course, you feel that the affair has to end, and you tell your lover so. Your lover's response is that, if the affair is ended, then he or she will pass on some damaging information about you to your superior; on the other hand, if the affair is continued, then he or she will speak well of you to your superior. Do you:

(a) end the affair, but say nothing to anyone else,
(b) continue the affair, or
(c) tell the whole story to your superior, and take the consequences?

Decision arising from the written code . . .
Your own decision . . .

CASE 7: THE PRICE

As a company director, you become aware that the price at which one of your company's products is being marketed is five times the full cost of its production, even after including labour costs, overheads, etc. The market will pay this price because there is no alternative product on the market. At a time of high economic inflation, you believe personally that it is wrong for the company to set such a high price for this product. So far as your board position is concerned, do you:

(a) do nothing,
(b) argue within the board for a considerable reduction in the price of the product, and be prepared to resign from the board if they do not agree with you, or
(c) accept a compromise with a small price reduction?

Decision arising from the written code . . .
Your own decision . . .

CASE 8: THE RECRUIT

As a middle manager, you need to recruit a new employee from outside the organization. There are three suitable candidates:

(a) a very bright graduate, who you feel might pose a challenge to your own position in the firm,
(b) a less able, but adequate, graduate, who is known to you as a militant political activist, or
(c) a mediocre, but attractive, member of the opposite sex.

Which one do you appoint?

Decision arising from the written code . . .
Your own decision . . .

CASE 9: THE ROGUES

You are one of several colleagues at work who need to travel a distance in your own cars from time to time to undertake tasks at an outpost of the business, and you are all able to claim travel expenses for these journeys on a mileage basis. It has been the common practice for many years among your colleagues to claim mileage for a distance of five miles more than is actually covered, and they want you to do the same otherwise their dishonesty is likely to be revealed. Do you:

(a) do the same as your colleagues,
(b) claim the accurate mileage, or
(c) try to persuade your colleagues to switch to the accurate mileage, but agree with what they eventually decide?

Decision arising from the written code . . .
Your own decision . . .

CASE 10: THE DRINKS

As director of a small company which runs a number of off-licence drinks stores, you are involved in arranging a visit to your premises by the local Member of Parliament, so that they might become more conversant with the operations of the company. It is suggested that at the end of the visit they should be presented with a gift in the form of a crate containing some of your merchandise worth over £100, not in respect of any particular favours asked, but generally to keep the MPs well-disposed towards the company. You are aware that they might be required to declare a gift of this value in the House of Commons 'Register of Members' Interests'. Do you:

(a) agree that the gift be made,
(b) try to persuade your colleagues to make no gift, or
(c) try to persuade your colleagues to make just a token gift of, say, a single bottle of wine?

Decision arising from the written code . . .
Your own decision . . .

Summary chart for BEG

Case	Title	Decision arising from written code	Your own decision	Whether agreement is 'Y' or 'N'
1	Criminals			
2	Applicant			
3	Fire			
4	Drug			
5	Confidentiality			
6	Affair			
7	Price			
8	Recruit			
9	Rogues			
10	Drinks			

Total number of 'Y's, multiplied by 10

Appendix II

Essay questions set in recent years on the Society and Management course at Bradford University

CHAPTER 1 INTRODUCTION

1 'Modern management is conducted increasingly on the rim, rather than at the hub, of the wheel of an organization.' Discuss.

CHAPTER 2 THE CURRENT CORPORATE, CAPITALIST ECONOMY

1 Examine how far the Iron Law of Population propounded by the Rev. Thomas Malthus can be observed in the world today. Make particular reference to the situations in at least two different countries.

2 Trace the development in British history of companies established by Royal Charter.

3 'Limited liability is a distortion of the free enterprise economy necessary for the promotion of commercial development.' Discuss.

4 To what extent has the privatization programme of the 1980s reduced the level of state involvement in business in the UK?

5 Trace the development of government intervention in the business market of the UK during the twentieth century?

6 Trace the main legal, social and technical developments affecting British business companies during the nineteenth century.

7 How much influence do shareholders in public limited companies in the UK have in the running of those organizations?

8 Give a historical outline of the changing pattern of ownership of the UK iron and steel industry.

9 Examine the cases for and against the Bank of England becoming totally independent of HM Government. What would you recommend?

10 'The economy of the UK would collapse if shareholders' liability were not limited.' Discuss.

11 How important was the impact on British commercial development of the events involving the South Sea Company in 1720-1?

CHAPTER 3 BUSINESS AND GOVERNMENT

1 Consider what aspects of the development of the European Community since 1984–5 are likely to have the greatest effects on UK-based businesses, and why.

2 Who is Mr Thomas Dawson? Examine how far his constitutional position is anomalous.

3 Suppose that the main road outside the factory where you are works manager is a trunk road. There have recently been several accidents on this road involving vehicles turning into, or out of, the factory, and it is believed that improved streetlighting would reduce the risk of such accidents. Describe how you would attempt to resolve the problem.

4 Describe the opportunities open to a business manager in the UK for making representations about matters of public policy.

5 Describe how the demand for macro-economic regulation in the European Economic Community has developed in response to economic and monetary failure.

6 Describe the relationship between government and Parliament in the UK.

7 'The European Monetary System is a greater infringement of national sovereignty than the Common Market.' Discuss.

8 Describe the ministerial structure within HM's Government, and the relationship between ministers at different levels.

9 Discuss the value of petitions as a means of making representations to public authorities.

10 Describe some of the implications for businesses in the UK of the changes proposed by the European Community taking effect in 1992.

11 Describe the scope of assistance which a British Member of Parliament may provide for a firm with premises within his constituency.

12 What are the main obstacles preventing the establishment of a common internal market within the European Community? What measures has the European Commission proposed for surmounting them?

13 What assistance can Members of the European Assembly (MEPs) give to firms located in their constituencies?

14 How far are local authorities in the UK hampered by current legislation in their attempts to compete commercially?

15 To what extent are local authorities in the UK independent of HM Government?

16 To what extent should Members of Parliament represent their constituents, their parties, some pressure groups or vested interests, or themselves?

17 How effective is the Confederation of British Industry in making representations to HM Government on behalf of British industry? Illustrate your answer by reference to particular cases.

18 '1992': more Hype than Reality?

CHAPTER 4 BUSINESS AND LAW

1 How far are the best interests of a UK company served by the full-time employment of a legal specialist or specialists rather than using independent professional lawyers on an *ad hoc* basis?

2 'With greater understanding by managers of the English system of administering justice, business decisions will be much enhanced.' Discuss.

3 Bad Co. Ltd owe Mr Creditor (a plumber) £3,000 for works performed by Mr Creditor. The invoice was rendered some six months ago. Advise Mr Creditor on how he may recover this sum in a lawful manner.

4 'The legal pitfalls of business continue to become deeper and more numerous' (Managing Legal Costs – CBI). Discuss the salient features of the legal system which are likely to be encountered in recovering from these pitfalls.

5 Describe for a business manager those features of the English courts' structure and practice which should be taken into consideration when his firm is either: (a) involved in a dispute about a contract, or (b) facing prosecution for allegedly selling goods bearing false trade descriptions.

6 Describe the structure of the system of courts of law in England and Wales, explaining the different functions of different courts.

7 Describe in detail some development in an aspect of the law of England and Wales which has been of significance for business companies since 1870.

8 Smith seeks your advice in connection with a proposed business venture. His friend Jones has proposed that the two of them should go into the car hire business, Jones providing £20,000 and Smith £10,000 as capital, each participating fully in the running of the business but with voting and profit-sharing in capital ratios. Jones is indifferent as to the choice of legal vehicle as between the company and partnership forms. Smith is attracted by the suggestion but needs to be reassured as to the better legal vehicle to achieve his concerns, which are as follows:

(a) He would like to be assured of his right to run the firm during his lifetime without, as he puts it, 'being given the push'.

(b) Because of Jones's opportunistic character (which leads him into making a wide variety of business transactions), it is essential that the company or partnership should have no liability outside the car hire business.

(c) He would like to have the right to expel Jones should the latter fail to devote full-time attention to the car hire business, become unfit mentally or physically to continue in the business or be convicted of any crime involving dishonesty.

What advice are you able to offer Smith?

9 How far, and in what way, can decisions of courts in England and Wales be overridden by judgments of European Courts?

10 Consider how an understanding of the system of administering justice in civil and criminal cases might inform the response of a business manager to a threat of legal action.

CHAPTER 5 BUSINESS AND ETHICS

1 What is business ethics? Why should businesses seek to practise ethical standards in their operations?

2 Give an account of the Prisoners' Dilemma. Can the Dilemma arise in real life business situations? If so, how should it be overcome?

3 'The possibility of business becoming more ethical is bound up with the possibility of its professionalization.' Comment.

4 'All's fair in love and war.' Is this also true of business?

5 The board of directors of a pharmaceutical company is faced with deciding whether to continue marketing a drug which independent studies have indicated may, in some cases, have fatal side-effects. What ethical considerations may have a bearing on the role played by an individual director in this situation?

6 Discuss the ethical, economic and environmental considerations involved in making aid to less developed countries dependent on whether they officially encourage birth control for their people.

CHAPTER 6 BUSINESS AND FINANCIAL AND FISCAL INSTITUTIONS

1 What expenses are allowable against a company's liability for corporate taxation in the UK? To what extent does this include charitable donations?

2 Assess the implications for corporate management of the growth in institutional investment.

3 Describe the obligations of businesses in relation to the Inland Revenue.

4 Describe the functions of merchant banks in relation to individual business companies.

5 What considerations would lead a private company in the UK to seek

public limited status? Describe in detail the steps to be taken in making this change.

CHAPTER 7 BUSINESS AND TECHNOLOGY

1 'Computers and telecommunications have transformed the financial world in the last ten years. The two key developments have been the speed of communications and access to enormous data bases.' Expand on this statement and explain how these two developments have improved the efficiency of the financial markets.

2 Assume that you are the financial director of a large retail organization. Explain how modern developments in computing might be used to improve the credit control facilities within your organization, particularly in relation to credit given, credit taken and control of credit amounts owing to your organization.

3 To what extent has the pattern of dealing in the world's stock exchanges been affected by the introduction of new technology?

4 Describe in detail how some aspect of modern technology has had an impact on business and commerce.

5 'The modern revolution in communications technology is making the world a safer place.' Discuss.

6 How may inventors of technical developments in the UK now realise the commercial potential of their inventions?

7 'It is in the knowledge industry that Britain has its greatest long-term potential' (T. Stonier, The Wealth of Information 1983: 148). Discuss this assertion and its implications for this country's future economic development.

8 Describe the application of computers and/or telecommunications to one of the following areas:
(a) electronic funds transfer
(b) financial data bases
(c) corporate wide accounting systems
(d) expert systems
Describe how the system works and discuss the possible effects of these developments on the financial system in the UK.

9 Describe how some particular technical invention in the last 40 years found its way from the original inventor(s) to the general market.

10 Outline the main areas of conflict and co-operation between unions and management over the introduction of new technology. Consider appropriate procedures for resolving any differences.

CHAPTER 9 BUSINESS AND PUBLIC RELATIONS

1 Discuss the role of public relations in the modern organization. Why is it seen to be a topic of increasing importance in the 1990s?
2 How can the works manager of a local factory most effectively develop good relations with representatives of the news media? Why should he or she do so?
3 'The freedom of the press is too precious to be restrained other than by the laws of libel.' Discuss.
4 Write a press release concerning a news item that has actually arisen at your place of work.
5 Describe how a business organization can benefit from the services of a public relations practitioner. Give examples.

CHAPTER 10 BUSINESS AND THE PHYSICAL ENVIRONMENT

1 'A clean environment and a high quality of life are incompatible with population growth and a truly free market economy.' Discuss.
2 'World economic forces threaten the future of civilized human existence.' Discuss.

References

Bentham, Jeremy (1781–5) *The Commonplace Book*, quoted in *The Works of Jeremy Bentham*, vol. X, ed. Bowring, J. (1962), New York: Russell & Russell.

Boswell, J. (1791) *Life of Johnson* (L. F. Powell's revision (1934) of G. B. Hill's edition (1887)), Oxford: Clarendon Press.

Churchill, Sir Winston (1956) *A History of the English-Speaking Peoples*, vol II: *The New World*, London: Cassell.

Churchill, Sir Winston (1957) *A History of the English-Speaking Peoples*, vol III: *The Age of Revolution*, London: Cassell.

Corfield, Sir Kenneth (1985) 'Managers for the 21st Century', The second E.G. Edwards Lecture, University of Bradford.

Davies, H. and Holdcroft, D. (1991) *Jurisprudence – Texts and Commentary*, London: Butterworth.

Fleming, I. (1955) *Casino Royale*, London: Pan Books.

Jefkins, F. (1987) *Public Relations for your Business*, London: Mercury Books.

Jolly, W.P. (1976) *Lord Leverhulme*, London: Constable.

Jones, G.P., and Pool, A.G. (1940) *A Hundred Years of Economic Development in Great Britain (1840–1940)*, London: Duckworth.

Joshi, H. (ed.) (1989) *The Changing Population of Britain*, Oxford: Basil Blackwell.

MacIntyre, A. (1967) *A Short History of Ethics*, London: Routledge & Kegan Paul.

Mackenzie, A. Slidell (1844) *Life of Stephen Decatur, a Commodore in the Navy of the United States*, Boston: Library of American Biography.

Malthus, T.R. (1798) *Essay on the Principle of Population*; an enlarged and amended edition appeared in 1807.

Malthus, T.R. (1815) *An Inquiry into the Nature and Progress of Rent*.

Mill, J.S. (1859) *On Liberty*.

Montesquieu, Baron Charles de (1748) *De L'Esprit des Lois*.

Pearce, D. (1991) *Corporate Responsibility and the Environment*, published by British Gas plc.

Ricardo, David (1817) *The Principles of Political Economy and Taxation*; recent edition published by Dent (London) in the Everyman's Library, 1969.

Smith, Adam (1776) *An Inquiry into the Nature and Causes of the Wealth of Nations*; recent edition published by Dent (London) in the Everyman's Library, 1958.

Index